THE COUPON QUEEN SAYS:

I spend ten dollars at the supermarket for an entire week's shopping for my family of three, including a supply of paper products and health and beauty aids. The cashier rings fifty to sixty dollars on the register but after coupons are deducted from my overflowing shopping cart, I pay only ten dollars or less. How can I do this?

It's really very simple. I use free coupons for specific products or grocery items of my choice such as fresh fruit, vegetables, cheese and meat. I pay only sales tax. The coupons are the end product of a game called REFUNDING.

And I'm not going to keep it a secret. My methods are all described right here in this book. Help yourself!

ASK THE COUPON QUEEN

MARY ANNE HAYES

PUBLISHED BY POCKET BOOKS NEW YORK

Another *Original* publication of POCKET BOOKS

 POCKET BOOKS, a Simon & Schuster division of
GULF & WESTERN CORPORATION
1230 Avenue of the Americas, New York, N.Y. 10020

Copyright © 1979 by Mary Anne Hayes

ISBN: 0-671-83349-9

First Pocket Books printing November, 1979

10 9 8 7 6 5 4 3 2 1

Trademarks registered in the United States and other countries.

Printed in the U.S.A.

Dedicated
to
Mom,
who survived bottomless
boxes of rice
and
cans without labels

Author's Note

Please note that all coupons, qualifiers, and other illustrations in this book are reproduced solely for the purpose of illustration and as an example of the kinds of promotional items that can be found in stores, newspapers, and other places. These illustrations DO NOT represent actual offers and should not be used by the reader as such.

All reproductions of the actual offers shown on the coupons herewith have been marked VOID; they will not be honored by any retailer or manufacturer.

Contents

Introduction

by Mary Anne's Mother

One day Mary Anne was a little girl refusing to eat spinach and, the next day, she became the sensational coupon queen, teaching the nation, including her own mother, how to shop for groceries on a shoestring. Mary Anne was always thrifty, splurging only on bubble gum machines, a habit she finally outgrew (to the dentist's delight).

I thought I knew everything about shopping from college home economics courses and years of practical experience. I purchased store brands to save a few pennies, avoided impulse buying, shopped on a full stomach, faithfully clipped out and redeemed seven-cents cash-off coupons and continued comparison shopping even after the gas crisis. Yet my own grocery bill continued to soar even though I served plain meals, practically eliminating snacks, desserts, and treats from my shopping list in a vain attempt to cut corners. When the large, economy size capsized my budget, I switched to smaller sizes, but that resulted in more frequent trips to the supermarket.

Then my teen-aged daughter discovered a shopping technique that was simple, original, legal, tax-free, and which actually enabled her to shop and leave her pocketbook at home! No matter how high supermarket prices skyrocket, Mary Anne still feeds her family of three on ten dollars a week. The ex-spinach hater now savors ready-to-serve vegetable casseroles smothered in butter, cream, or Hollandaise sauce. Frankly, I could never afford to try the fancy vegetables that Mary Anne obtains free or for a fraction of their retail cost.

Mary Anne earned her title when she astonished the nation on CBS-TV in February 1978 by ringing up a full cart of groceries to the tune of $71.71 in a New Jersey supermarket but, after coupons were subtracted, actually owing only $7.19. Since then she has passed the coupon endurance test by surviving repeated royal battles with registers at various supermarkets for *Family Circle*, *Lady's Circle*, *The Star*, *People Magazine*, and a myriad of newspapers from coast to coast. She has amazed audiences on the "Mike Douglas Show," "Mid-Day Live" with Bill Boggs, "America Alive" with Jack Linkletter, Walter Cronkite's national news program, "Women's World," the "David Susskind Show," and news commentary and television talk shows in New York, Philadelphia, and Washington, D.C.

Mary Anne, the undisputed Coupon Queen, lectures at consumer education seminars in schools and colleges throughout the state of New Jersey. She has appeared on over 250 radio talk shows and now broadcasts her own syndicated program on which she gives her choice of the refund of the week as well as refunding tips to beginners and old pros.

The Coupon Queen has become the empress of the supermarket and an idol to over fifty thousand subscribers of her publication, *Dollars Daily*, which is a chronicle featuring more than two hundred current new offers each month. After only a brief time in refunding, the Queen's students successfully branch off into challenging shopping ventures of their own with the aid of coupons.

Dollars Daily has spread through the nation like wildfire with its sure method of combating inflation and beating the system. Now her book, *Ask the Coupon Queen*, gives step-by-step instructions so that you may slash your grocery bill and perhaps vacation in Bermuda with your profits.

Mary Anne breaks all traditional shopping rules that I grew up with and yet manages to exchange mundane menus for gourmet meals while banking dollars daily.

Ask the Coupon Queen teaches you how to put refunding into practice so that you too may win supermarket duels with the register.

If I sound like a proud mother, it's only because I am.

Frances R. Calabria

1
The Centsational Story

Mary Anne Discovers Cash in Trash

I started refunding when I was a teenager and needed gas for the car. I remember the countdown to my seventeenth birthday when I could obtain my driver's license, and I visualized myself cruising down country roads in my yellow bird, an economical Toyota®. Then I learned the driving facts of life. Gas was expensive, and even the economy car that squeezed thirty miles to the gallon burned too much gas for my limited income earned by Saturday night baby-sitting.

One day, I happened to notice a message on a package of rice that Mom brought home from the store: "Send two box bottoms with the Universal Product Code, and receive $1.00." I scanned the bottom of the package and for the first time observed a small square with squiggly lines and a number of digits preceded by the letters *UPC*, so I guessed this was what the company wanted. I didn't know what this strange pattern indicated or why it suddenly appeared on that particular package. Lucky for me, Mom had another half-used package of rice inside the brown cabinet that used to be a gray cabinet. (This is a standing joke in our family, because whenever my brother Pat, or I, needed anything and could not find it, Mom would describe its whereabouts in the same way.) The second package did not have the same offer printed or the UPC number, so I doubted whether I would be eligible to receive a dollar back. I peeled off the paper portion of both box bottoms before Mom could cook the rice and discard the packaging.

Whenever I must make a decision and am concerned about the outcome, I remember Grandpa Andy's sage pearls of wisdom, "Columbus took a chance," and gain the needed courage to go ahead. Sure enough, like Columbus, I made a discovery. I received my first refunding dollar weeks later; I could barely recall the origin of that crisp new bill. Wow! I learned a priceless secret. Refunding was a lot easier than baby-sitting for a whole hour and guaranteed fuel for extra mileage. It took only a moment to address the envelope and jot down my name and address on the mail-in certificate from the specially marked package. Our rural mailbox was as close as the front gate, so I never had to leave the warmth of my home to earn money. Now I could extend my budget at my own time and convenience and regain my lost date night. (Baby-sitting had really put a dent in my social life, cooling Saturday night fever and eliminating all possibilities of attendance at school dances, the Senior Prom and New Year's Eve parties.)

I asked Mom to serve that particular brand of rice more often and tried to bribe her with special recipes from an international cookbook collection gathering dust on the bookshelves. However, I soon learned that families do not live by rice alone. I started an extensive search for refund offers in every store I entered, in newspapers, and in magazines, and I turned the brown cabinet inside out seeking additional specially marked packages.

I discovered refund offers on all types of products, ranging from first-aid creme to cosmetics to antifreeze. My sunny Toyota sparkled from coats of free self-polishing wax and smoothly glided to Brookdale Community College when treated with refundable radiator flush, brake fluid, gas, and antifreeze conditioners. I recruited my brother Pat's muscle power and automotive know-how when necessary, convincing him to change the snow tires that I now could afford with refunding profits. Whenever I spotted a cash-back deal for any automotive product, I seized it. Pat demonstrated how to utilize the item and received a duplicate for his own car. I began to understand about cooling-system maintenance and found dozens of products on the market designed to improve automobiles' performance and create that new car sheen. I can honestly say that refunding taught me how to take proper care of my automobile and enabled me to obtain free labor to do so.

All that was necessary was digging out the refund, investing in the product, mailing proofs of purchase, and impatiently waiting for the mailman's arrival with a cash return. When I became a serious refunder, I earned enough money not only for gas but also for my automobile insurance premium.

I was completely hooked on the refunding game and loved to tag along on Mom's shopping expeditions to see what goodies I could find. Mom was willing to vary the menu as long as I took a solemn oath to taste the product that I begged her to buy. I originally was a finicky eater, but when there was money in the deal, I soon learned to try new products with an open mind and often surprised my taste buds. For example, Mom tried to get us to eat plain spinach for years. She used Popeye to overcome my older brother's resistance, but I wouldn't budge and refused to touch the stuff. Now I found myself going on a creamed spinach binge and loving it. Mom never bought vegetables with special sauces but agreed to my request when I wanted to receive a buck back. The flavorsome cream softened the taste of spinach, and it was delicious. Even after the refund expired, Mom continued to serve my favorite vegetable, and I saved the labels on speculation. Of course, I eventually collected on every one of them.

Pat loved snooping around the brown cabinet, which now could rival Fibber McGee's closet, over-stuffed with edible refundable treasures that we otherwise would not splurge on. At that time, I was concerned only with money-back offers and skipped those for free food coupons since they were valueless to me. It wasn't until I was married and in full charge of menu planning that I took an active interest in coupons.

When Baby Jimmy arrived during my first year of marriage, I had the additional challenge of juggling the budget to accommodate jars of baby food and boxes of disposable diapers. During the sugar crunch, when the price of Jimmy's favorite chocolate chip cookie mix leaped from twenty-nine cents to ninety-nine cents, I decided it was time for a quick and easy coupon action plan.

At first my husband, Jim, thought my label collection was ridiculous. He approved of coin and stamp collections, but couldn't see how labels that were discarded by people every day could return money. He wasn't alone in his initial mistrust of my hobby. Friends advised me to stop squandering time and postage on advertising gimmicks that would never bring cash back. However, I stuck to my guns, because I knew the truth and had already collected on many refunds. By now, my grocery bill had diminished as my obsession for free food coupons grew.

Jim objected to clutter, and when he arrived home earlier than usual from his sheet metal job to discover me knee deep in labels, forms, and exchange letters, he decided it was time to help me organize. I concentrated on methods of organization so that refunding could become a one-hour-a-day avocation when baby napped. Jim gathered together carpentry tools and lumber to design a massive desk promising to house my refunding clutter. The desk had a smooth, broad top, perfect for envelope addressing, and it provided adequate storage space for refund forms, labels, and correspondence. My most severe critic was now my ally with complete faith in my ability to slash supermarket bills. Since actually enjoying gourmet meals on five labels a day, Jim enlisted in my label-saving campaign, reminding *me*, the great refunder, to retrieve every qualifier that came our way. Once we were at a pizza parlor, and the waitress tried to discard an empty potato chip wrapper after she poured the chips on our plate. Jim reminded me that we paid for the packaging as well as the contents and that there was a current refund on that particular brand. A confused waitress mumbled to herself as she walked away, minus the wrapper.

Nonrefunders can never understand the instant insanity caused whenever a refunder visualizes qualifiers going up in smoke. Only those who have received their first dollar back can empathize with refunding hobbyists' never-ending search to match labels and refund forms. Refunding is a contagious condition, lasting forever. Once a refunder, always a refunder.

After you have received that first return, you absolutely cannot stop; it's addictive. From the time I received my first dollar back, I located refunding pen pals of all ages in every state, including Alaska and Hawaii. Sometimes I long for the days when I had time to chat by mail with all refunding buddies. We exchanged information gleaned from supermarkets, variety discount stores, automotive departments, appliance centers, shoe stores, pharmacies, local newspapers, magazines, and even restaurants. It was impossible for one person to know about all refund offers available throughout the country, so I started gathering information and compiling lists of current refunding opportunities sent to me by fellow refunders.

Most refund promotions are good throughout the United States. Occasionally, a refund offer is available to a limited test area only. Usually the form will state which geographical location will be honored for the promotion, but in rare instances it is omitted from the refund form or newspaper write-up. The manufacturer usually returns your request and qualifiers at expense to themselves, which reduces their refund budgets. Not good news for refunders! I think all manufacturers should state whether the offer is limited or not.

With Jim's encouragement I put these tips all together in the very first issue of *Dollars Daily*, mimeographed in October 1977. (Jim gets credit for the title of the publication. It's his description of what the mail carrier brought every day.) We hand-churned one hundred copies on a manual machine that had a stubborn mind of its own. I mailed the paper to refunding buddies, who in turn sent me new information for the forthcoming issue of *Dollars Daily*. It seemed that everyone had a friend interested in refunding, because my subscription list doubled the next month. Soon two hundred copies rumbled out of the antiquated machine. We were sold out, and I barely rescued one copy for my own use.

2
Refund Fever

The Nation Jumps on the Refunding Bandwagon

A local New Jersey reporter heard about *Dollars Daily* from one of my subscribers and wanted to see for herself how my system worked. She asked to accompany me on a shopping trip in order to help readers benefit from my shopping prowess. Other local newspapers picked up the story, and I felt as if I had really hit the big time when a photographer from the *New York Daily News* braved a snowstorm to find his way to my mobile home. Eventually, the Associated Press spread the refunding word to papers throughout the nation. The CBS television news staff read one of these articles and asked if Arnold Diaz, a very handsome New York-based reporter, could come along on one of my shopping trips at the supermarket. The rest is refunding history. I purchased $71.71 worth of groceries, but after coupons were subtracted, paid only $7.19 to the cashier. The CBS telephone lines were jammed with pleas for further information, and my name and address were flashed across the screen for two days. After the CBS bombardment of telephone inquiries, I returned to the supermarket the very next day for another quick shopping trip with Arnold Diaz.

Television cameras jammed my living room as I typed the next issue of *Dollars Daily* and tried to give viewers insight into the refunding game. At the supermarket Diaz scrutinized each coupon with the skill of an experienced supermarket checker. Although it took four hours to videotape, the actual news segment lasted only a few moments on television. With the thrill of a James Bond chase scene, we flew through the supermarket, racing with the clock, as cameras followed my grocery choices and Diaz led the quiz session. At 4:30 P.M., we were still in a New Jersey supermarket, but after a hurried trip to a local airport and a waiting helicopter, Diaz and my videotape were whisked to the CBS studio for transmission on the six o'clock news program.

The next week in February 1978, our post office faced two unforgettable blizzards. Snowdrifts mounted high through the Lakehurst streets, and trays of mail addressed to the Coupon Queen filled the post office. When Jim and I innocently stopped at the counter to ask if there was any mail, we saw a speechless postal employee with bulging eyes and an open mouth. We had hopefully anticipated a few hundred inquiries, but there suddenly appeared a giant cart barely accommodating fourteen trays of mail piled so high that the six-foot postal employee pushing the cart was completely hidden from sight. The postmaster proudly announced, "Now you've done it, Mary Anne. You received more mail than the entire area of Lakehurst, including the Naval Air Station." I laughed, thinking this was a practical joke since everyone in Lakehurst had seen my television debut.

I thumbed through the mail in the top tray, and sure enough every letter was addressed to the Coupon Queen. Trays of mail crammed the backseat of my loyal Toyota right to the roof; we couldn't see through the rearview window. We packed the trunk and still had to make another trip to pick up the remainder of one day's mail. That morning we immediately started opening fan mail but by nightfall had only skimmed through two hundred letters. Each tray contained approximately six hundred letters. We were getting nowhere fast and issued an urgent call for help. We resorted to the good old telephone to tell Mom to come down and see what her box of rice had started. We instructed her to bring along my brother and his wife, Nana, my uncle, cousins, Jim's entire family, and hitchhikers they could con into opening mail. As dawn approached, the weary troop had answered only one tray of mail. Our tiny mobile home just could not accommodate the next day's deluge. We were literally forced out of the trailer by overflowing mail. Jim, Baby Jimmy, and I moved to Mom's large house, where the dozens of mail trays that arrived daily could follow us and the family could continuously pitch in on staggered shifts to open, sort, and reply to inquiries.

I received gifts of perfume, herb seeds, plant hangers, offers to write newspaper and magazine articles, invitations to speak at every conceivable group meeting, and one offer my husband did not appreciate, a proposal of marriage.

We vowed not to return to the mobile home until every single letter was answered, and the volume of mail subsided. Walter Cronkite of CBS television fame did another video presentation of my now famous hobby, and refund fever spread throughout the country like wildfire. After three months at my mother's house, we unconditionally surrendered when the total volume of letters reached 100,000. We returned to Lakehurst, where mail continued to pour in on a daily basis, but we now were experienced in the fine art of handling mail.

Our next issue of *Dollars Daily*, published for the month of March 1978, had 10,000 subscribers. Our hand-operated mimeograph machine collapsed under pressure, and a new automatic model was required just to print thank-you letters to well-wishers congratulating me for successfully beating the system.

Dollars Daily was now a professionally printed tabloid requiring many hours of hard work. Jim was forced to leave his sheet metal job to assist in publishing it. We quickly learned about the printing trade and the skills of typesetting and layout. *Dollars Daily* contains dated information, and we couldn't afford to squander precious days waiting at the printer's for the job's completion. We worked around the clock, taking catnaps whenever possible. (I still don't remember what it's like to get a full night's sleep.) Sometimes I typed all night long, burning the midnight oil to meet an 8:00 A.M. deadline so that *Dollars Daily* would be ready to go to press.

It was physically impossible to hand address thousands of newspapers by the fifteenth of the month, our mailing date. Jim immediately had to locate and learn how to operate an addressograph. We had no previous publishing experience or frame of reference, so we worked out immediate problems to the best of our abilities as they arose, always keeping in mind the echo of Grandpa Andy's advice about Columbus. We made minor errors in those early publishing days, but we soon learned how to iron them out professionally. We still couldn't afford hired help, so we depended upon family volunteers, who came through like troopers. The big day finally arrived when our backlog of mail was sorted and reached a stage where we could handle it on a daily basis.

Dollars Daily continued to grow in leaps and bounds, and on its first anniversary in October 1978, our number of subscribers passed 50,000. My once-small hobby designed to stretch a dollar had turned into a business venture overnight. At twenty-one years of age, I was an employer directing employees older than myself.

Photographs of me and articles about my success story appeared in *Family Circle, Lady's Circle, The Star* and *People* magazines, and I was a frequent guest star on numerous radio and television talk shows.

Now I can laugh at my radio debut from my tiny kitchen in the trailer. A disc jockey from Newark, New Jersey, contacted me and told me to hold on to the telephone because he wanted to interview me over the air. "Don't hang up under any circumstances," he insisted. "I'll be right with you, but first a few words from my sponsor." Because his broadcast did not extend to Lakehurst, I could hear only his telephone voice and not the actual program. Little Jimmy was very young and apt to cry and ruin the broadcast, so I decided to heat his bottle and rock him to sleep while I held on tightly to the phone. The considerate baby took a full three-hour nap while I grew impatient with the disc jockey, who never returned to the phone. Finally, when the baby woke up from his nap, I decided it was time to hang up and forget the broadcast. I later discovered we were inadvertently disconnected and my line was busy because I was holding on to a dead phone. Since that unsuccessful radio debut, which incidentally was broadcast successfully the next day during Jimmy's nap time, I have spoken on approximately 250 local radio stations, ranging from sunny Pasadena to wintry Montreal. I now have my own syndicated weekly radio program and local cable television spot which offer my refund choice of the week and refunding tips.

No matter how busy I am or how fast the days fly by, I always spare a precious hour a day to turn magician and change a postage stamp with qualifier into a crisp dollar bill. When my brother, Pat, and I were children, Grandpa Andy would reward us with a half dollar mystically appearing by sleight of hand. He would appreciate the magic of refunding and my own special way of pulling dollars out of thin air. It's a lot easier to pull a coupon from an envelope than a rabbit from a hat.

3

Mary Anne's Grocery List

$120 Worth of Groceries for 79¢

One summer we rented a beach house at the Jersey shore. I can resist everything except temptation: during the first week of our vacation, I overspent our money at the casino there. In addition, we were entertaining guests, and extra company means extra meals and snacks. Sultry summer days demand a constant flow of long, cool drinks. So on this particular shopping trip to a new seaside supermarket I was faced with duplex challenges of minimal funds and a houseful of hungry and thirsty guests. I was determined not to skimp on entertainment but to focus my menu around free coupons with a bare minimum of cost.

We needed sugar-free items because bikini weather caused everyone, except the baby and the puppy, to become diet conscious. Summertime diet pledges fade more rapidly than New Year's Eve resolutions. Our family is partial to Italian cookery so we casually sip diet drinks while munching lasagna.

As refunders glance through this shopping list, they will recognize many items offering current refunds although original offers bringing free coupons for our beach house vacation expired several years ago. Refunds, like all good things, eventually come to a halt. However, manufacturers constantly offer new promotions for the same favorites when new entries hit the scene. That is why I must stress the importance of filing systems and an on-going label-saving campaign. Even at the beach house when relaxed guests attempted to discard candy wrappers out of habit, I would gently remind them, "Hold it! Those labels will pay for my next vacation."

This is how my chain of free groceries continues to grow. A plastic wrap offers a coupon for potato chips; later the chips offer another coupon or cash. It reminds me of the old-fashioned wedding chain of my Italian ancestry. Mom invited second cousins to her wedding that she actually never had the pleasure of meeting simply because her mother-in-law attended their weddings. You just couldn't break the chain. Wedding reception sizes multiplied out of proportion, and an invitation had to be produced at the door, since gate crashing became a popular Saturday night pastime. Those were the beer-and-sandwich weddings Guido Panzini (alias Pat Harrington) reminisces about, where everyone had fun but no one knew the bride! Refunding chains grow in the same way as long as you save the labels. One refunding promotion leads to another, and soon you are receiving money back for items you originally obtained free for the purchase of a companion product. This is a copy of my seaside shopping list. We used every item that summer, but the case of Pepsi, and the bag of ice disappeared first. Remember, I had a coupon for each specific item on this list plus several others for grocery items of my choice, which were utilized for produce and meat.

$120 SHOPPING LIST

Cubex ® ice cubes
1 case Diet Pepsi® (24 cans)
8 qt cannister Funny Face Lemonade®
24 oz. Wyler's Punch® drink mix
Canada Dry® ginger ale
Nestea® iced-tea mix
Maxwell House® coffee
Sanka® instant coffee
Decaf® instant coffee
Sprinkle Sweet® sugar substitute
Milk (Drakes'® cake coupon)
Milk (Nabisco® coupon)
Morningstar Farms® grilled sausage
Aunt Jemima® maple-flavored pancake syrup
Aunt Jemima® whole wheat pancake mix
Buttermilk pancake mix
Quaker® puffed rice cereal
Hotel Bar® whipped butter
Post® Raisin Bran
Chiffon® soft stick margarine
Bright and Early® frozen orange juice
Birds Eye® frozen orange juice
Minute Maid® orange juice, refrigerated
Nabisco Chips Ahoy® chocolate chip cookies
Welch's® frozen jelly donuts
Betty Crocker® brownie mix
Betty Crocker® cake mix
Pillsbury® frosting
Gold Medal® flour
Lender's® plain frozen bagels
Lender's® raisin and honey frozen bagels
Eggs

Cool-Whip® non-dairy whipped topping
Reddi Wip® instant whipped cream
Hunt's Snack Pak
Royal® instant pudding
Del Monte® raisins
Good Humor® ice cream bars
Ice Cream (Reddi Wip® coupon)
Bounty® eight-bar package coconut candy
Nestlé's® 6-bar chocolate candy
Skittle's® fruit chews candy
Libby's® chunky mixed fruit
Dole® sliced pineapple
Del Monte® fruit cocktail
Libby's® canned tomato juice
Adolph's® meat tenderizer
Salad Crispins® food salad topping
Pride of the Farm® Ketchup
Kosciusko® mustard
Hunt's® ketchup
Hunt's® Manwich sauce
Low-calorie salad dressing
Blue-cheese salad dressing
Seven Seas® Italian salad dressing
Adolph's® gravy mix
Buitoni® high protein spaghetti
2 lbs. spaghetti (Ragú® coupon)
Creamettes® elbow macaroni
Cheese (Sunshine® coupon)
Grated parmesan cheese (Oscar Mayer® coupon)
Mrs. T.'s® pierogies
Canned chili
Canned baked beans
Hot dog rolls
Hamburger rolls

Marcal® toilet tissue four-roll package
Marcal® paper towels
Scott® paper towels
Teri® paper towels
Marcal® hankies
Marcal® fluff-out tissues (three boxes)
Saran Wrap®
Glad® extra-wide plastic wrap
Glad® freezer wrap
Glad® sandwich bags
Hefty® lawn bags
Hefty® large waste bags
Vanish® toilet bowl cleaner
Ajax® king-size dishwashing liquid
All® concentrated detergent
Earth Born® shampoo—strawberry essence
Dial® roll-on deodorant
Man-Power® deodorant
Jergen's® soap
Scented soap
Tender Vittles® cat food
Square Meal® cat food
Meow Mix® cat food
Friskies® puppy food
Gaines® dog biscuits for small dogs
Lolli-Pups® dog treats
Libby's® sauerkraut
Del Monte® peas and carrots
Green Giant® cream style corn
Green Giant® three bean salad
Green Giant® whole kernel corn
Del Monte® asparagus
Redpack® canned tomatoes
Betty Crocker® potato buds

Frozen french fried potatoes ($1 coupon on potatoes)
Holloway House® baked beans
Veg-All® mixed vegetables
Ragú® Thick and Zesty spaghetti sauce
Aunt Millie's® pepper and sausage-flavored sauce
Ragú® pizza sauce
Hunt's® prima salsa sauce
Ragú® Italian cooking sauce
Chicken (Ragú coupon)
Chopped beef (Borden's® cheese coupon)
Frankfurters (Hydrade®)
Sirloin steak (Dr Pepper® coupon)
Minute steaks (Johnson & Johnson® $3 coupon on any
    grocery item)
Turkey (Butterball®)
Fresh Jersey tomatoes, onions, peppers, and escarole
    (produce coupons)
Fresh Jersey peaches (Royal® coupon for fruit)
Lettuce (Marie's® salad dressing coupon)
Watermelon (Borden® coupon)
Gorton's® breaded shrimp
Carnation® frozen shrimp
Taste O' Sea® seafood platter
Taste O' Sea® clam platter
Taste O' Sea® shrimp platter
Buitoni® frozen pizza
John's® frozen pizza
Buitoni® manicotti
Howard Johnson® clamburgers
Red L® quiche lorraine frozen appetizers
Freshen-up® gum
Datril® aspirin substitute
Colgate® toothpaste
Scope® mouthwash

4

Get Ready

How Can You Cash in on This Great Giveaway?

The name of the game is refunding, and you always collect on GO. Do you realize that you are discarding hundreds of dollars annually in the trash barrel? Don't ever discard an empty can or jar without stripping its label, or valuable food dollars will go up in smoke.

Dear Coupon Queen:

Is refunding new? I never heard of it before I saw you on television. If it was here, how come I didn't hear about it? I don't live in a vacuum.

Pudding Head

Dear Pudding Head:

Refunding is not new. Mom's favorite childhood memento was a blue glass Shirley Temple pitcher that she received for cereal box tops. Captain Video watches, Tom Mix mugs, and coupons for free Ivory Flakes® for new brides are all refunds of the past. Originally, refund premiums were most often offered

*by cereal and detergent manufacturers. Ever buy a
package of laundry detergent and find a glass or towel
in it? This is a form of refudning. Nana saved red roses
from LaRosa® spaghetti and Octagon® coupons for
premiums. Today's refunding is quick and easy to keep
pace with today's fast living. Just one cookie or frozen
cake box top will bring a buck back. You don't have to
wait until you have collected a quantity of box tops.*

*Maybe refund promotions are not heavily adver-
tised. I don't know why you never heard of them before
or still aren't aware of the multitude of offers floating
around. Maybe if I hadn't noticed the mail-in
certificate on that box of rice, I too still might be
unaware of refunding. Don't linger on the past and
labels gone with the wind. Just start saving them today.*

I spend ten dollars at the supermarket for an entire
week's shopping for my family of three, including a
supply of paper products and health and beauty aids.
The cashier rings fifty to sixty dollars on the register
but after coupons are deducted from my overflowing
shopping cart, I pay only ten dollars or less. How can I
do this?

It's really very simple. I use free coupons for
specific products or grocery items of my choice, such as
fresh fruit, vegetables, cheese, and meat. I pay only
sales tax. The coupons are the end products of a game
called *Refunding*.

Refunding is the process of sending labels, box
tops, and other proofs of purchase to the manufacturer
or clearinghouse for cash, gifts, and coupons for free
merchandise.

Refunding is not a money-back guarantee that you
receive for being dissatisfied with the product. You

receive cash back or free coupons whether you like the item or not. Usually I enjoy the variety of top-quality, refundable products, but I willingly switch brands for bigger or better refunds.

Refund Offers

Actual refund offers can be found in newspapers, magazines, on specially marked packages, and in special-refunding publications like *Dollars Daily* (which lists over two hundred new offers each month), and on all types of store shelves, ranging from those in shoe stores to those in appliance centers. Wednesday or Thursday newspaper editions have supermarket specials advertised, as do Sunday supplements and all types of magazines. Sometimes special packaging has the refund offer actually printed on the wrapper.

Dollars Daily tries to point out which offers are regional whenever the manufacturer indicates the same on their offers.

Printed refund forms are not always required. Usually, the offer will state clearly whether you need the actual form or not. If there is no statement that the printed form is required, a plain piece of paper will suffice when requesting the refund, as long as you know where to mail the request. Once properly mailed, there's no way refunds won't come in. You'll be in the money with each wager of a postage stamp. Refund parleys really pay off because they are a sure thing for you and the company. You get paid for trying the product, and the manufacturer introduces new products and reacquaints you with former favorites hidden away on supermarket shelves.

Save *all* refund offers and mail-in certificates

whether or not you care to participate in the promotion. These printed offers are valuable and can be traded with other refunders. (*Dollars Daily*, for example, has a classified section advertising refund offers that its subscribers want to trade for other refund offers of their choice. Other local or special-interest periodicals may have the same. But again, make sure the offer is national if you're trading cross country.)

Where Are All the Refund Offers?

Beginners often claim they have never seen a refund offer form. Once you train your eyes to find them, you will discover them all over the place. One refunder admitted, "Now I can spot a refund a mile away!"

Do you have to buy junk foods? Do you have to buy products that you don't use? Judge for yourself at the sampling of random offers illustrated. Do you use any of these products, and what do you get for their labels?

Offers are often printed on specially marked packages containing the product.

FREE

Corning Ware

Petite 1½ Cup Saucepan with plastic cover with proof of purchase on any 6 French's Sauce and Gravy products. Suggested retail price $4.58.

Included with your FREE Petite Pan are details on special savings on other Corning products in the

Kitchen Collection '79

from **french's**

VOID

Save $2.00 up to on RALEIGH LIGHTS

VOID

OFFER EXPIRES DECEMBER 31, 1979

TAKE   ONE

$4.00 Worth of Groceries FREE.

$4.00 Coupon Offer by mail

SEE DETAILS ON REVERSE SIDE

VOID

UP TO

$3 CASH REFUND

VOID

FROM your Rainbow of KLEENEX Tissues

Qualifiers

When you mail your refund form, you must be sure to include the correct *qualifier*. The qualifier is the part of the packaging required by the company for the refund. This could be the box top or bottom, the Universal Product Code, proof-of-purchase seal, ingredient panel, entire label, or another designated portion of the packaging.

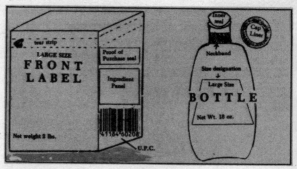

Reprinted from "Dollars Daily" Copyright © 1978.

Where to Find Your Qualifiers

Read the refund offer carefully. Whatever is requested is clearly identified on the product, except the UPC number, which most companies take for granted, but which everyone now understands and can easily recognize. For those who've never paid much attention to parts of packages before—a little "identi-kit" follows.

UPC (Universal
Product Code)

Purchase
Confirmation

Quality Seal

Net Weight

Proof of Purchase Seal
(In this example the UPC
has been included.)

Tear Off Strip

Box Top

Ingredient Panel

Box Bottom

Plastic Inner Liner
(from soda-bottle Cap)

Neck Band (from catsup)

Inner Seal

Label (soaked
from jar of
peanut butter)

Sample of a check redeemable for cash. This replica of a
cash-refund check is what the real thing looks like. Such
checks should be endorsed on the back and cashed as checks at
the bank—not at the supermarket. Some companies send
cash refunds in coins or bills, while others send checks.

CHRISTMAS ROAST

$2.00 Meat Offer
with Mama Ray's
DOWN HOME SAUCE

Mail-In Offer
See Back

Buy 2, Get 1 FREE

MAIL-IN OFFER

Garden Catsup

Buy 2 and get a coupon
for your next one

FREE

See Details on Back

Hang Tags

Example of a *complete deal*—everything that is called for to get your refund. First there is the official mail-in certificate. The front explains what the "deal" is. You must fill out the back, and include the piece of packaging called for—in this case the side name panel.

Sample of a free coupon or a substantial amount off on a product. Again, these are replicas—sent to you by the manufacturer for having completed a "deal" and sent in the proper qualifiers. In this case, the coupons are for the purchase of "companion" products. For example, Ragu® offered a free box of spaghetti, which would certainly go well with one of their sauces. Marie's® offered any chip item, in hopes perhaps that it would go well with or in a salad—or perhaps to induce customers to try Marie's® as a dip or part of a dip. Make sure to note that coupons for free groceries almost always have expiration dates.

These types of coupons are brought to the grocery store or supermarket, and are given in hopes you will try a new product. Thank You® Pudding was a new item in our grocery store. Our family had always used packaged puddings or the small individual cans. This was our first family-sized can of rice pudding—and we loved it. The Glad® Wrap coupon was a welcome sight since we are familiar with the product in our house. But there seems to be a lot of competition in the field of disposable bags and plastic wrap, so offers are frequently available.

Refund Offers Without Purchases

Some refund offers do not require that you actually purchase the product. They may require the code number or list of active ingredients. I guess they figure that if you pick up the product from the overcrowded supermarket shelves and study it, you deserve the refund and probably will try the product. Even if you don't purchase it then, you certainly will use the product when the free coupon arrives.

Both Top Job® and Oxydol® had current refunds requesting your name and address only. However, these trial offers appeared in various areas of the country at different times with special box number addresses for each location. Maybe you saw the free offers on your TV set as I did but could not copy the

address in time to participate in the offer. These cardboard backings indicate neither a mail-in certificate nor a purchase is necessary to receive your free coupon. Each company has so much faith in their product that they believe in the adage, "Try it, you'll like it!" And they're right!

Cash-offs

Cash-offs are *not* refund coupons. Cash-off coupons are usually for small amounts like seven or ten cents off a product. You bring the coupons to your grocer or store dealer to be redeemed when you purchase the articles.

Cash-offs should only be redeemed when you actually purchase the item at retail distributers. I do not use cash-off coupons. My grocery bills soared to an all-time high when I used them. I purchased expensive extras I didn't need just to get a few cents off the total price.

Cash-offs are cents-off coupons redeemed at the store when the item is purchased.

Most of these cents-off, or cash-off coupons are found in newspapers (about 55 percent of them), some in magazines (about 15 percent), and a few are found on or inside the product package (8 percent). The rest are either mailed or found in newspaper supplements. American shoppers redeemed $508 million worth of cash-offs in 1977, according to a survey conducted by A. C. Nielsen of TV rating fame. However, this represents only 5½ percent of the 46 billion cash-off coupons distributed by manufacturers.

I don't think that the average household can afford to redeem all cents-off coupons available, but you should judge the value of them yourself. Sometimes a cash-off is issued in conjunction with a refund offer, thereby offering a double saving. For example, Cycle® dog food gave a double coupon. Half could be separated on the perforated line for a fifty-cent cash-off when you buy your first product. Then the other half of the promotion was a refund offer for another free five- or ten-pound bag of the same dog food. In this case, the cash-off usage is justifiable. But you must have family cooperation, and my little Pekinese, Skippy (known to snitch Sandy's cat food), won't touch it. However, every dog has its own likes and dislikes. And even though Skippy wasn't particularly happy, I was glad to try a new product, as always, when the price is right.

Sometimes refund promotions are accompanied by cash-offs from generous sponsors, thereby giving the consumer a double savings. That's when a cash-off is really worth it.

If you choose to use the cash-offs, you must also put up with the hassle of organizing them for presentation to the cashier on demand and keeping close track of expiration dates as well. As for me, I'd rather refund.

Lately the newspapers have been full of million-dollar scandals about false cash-off redemption. Stores or store fronts fraudulently mail cash-offs on the pretense of selling the item to collect the value amount on the cash-off plus a handling charge without moving merchandise. Sometimes charities play a part in this fraud without their knowledge, and sometimes employees are instructed to cut out cash-off coupons from newspapers and magazines that are going back to the publisher and turn these in to the manager's office. Even contests are held to see which employee, individual, or charity can collect the largest quantity of cash-offs, which are then fraudulently redeemed.

Remember, when you read about coupon scandals, they are *not* referring to refunds. Perhaps companies will decide refund offers are a better way of reaching the consumer and having their products utilized since the offers are mailed directly to the consumer's home. Refunders certainly would never participate in these schemes. After all, why not use the free product?

Money-plus Offers

These are *not* refund offers. They may be placed on "Take One" pads at the supermarket and require several labels, but they always ask for a certain amount of cash to accompany the order. Please do *not* confuse money-plus offers with refunds. They may or may not be worth the cost to the buyer. Sometimes the manufacturers purchase the premiums in a huge quantity so

The value of a money-plus offer is in the eye of the beholder.

that they can offer it to customers at a savings. However, most refunders rarely use money-plus offers since we are in the business of making money and not spending it.

Never trade money-plus offers with fellow refunders and expect to receive cash or coupon refund forms in exchange. You may mark money-plus offers "Extra" and include them with your trade if you personally feel it is a good opportunity that you would like to share. Remember, these extras may bring your postage rate up, and you will have to pay for the privilege of mailing a perhaps undesired form.

When exchangers clearly state "No Junk," they usually are referring to money-plus offers, sweepstakes, or cash-offs. Many find value in these forms, but true refunders are solely interested in refund offers, not money-plus offers.

5

Refunding in a Shoe Box

How to Refund

Before mailing that first refund request, study the following instructions:

1. Save every label, food wrapper, and inner seal that you use. Even if there is not a refund right now, there probably will be one in the near future.
2. Purchase a supply of the least expensive envelopes you can find and a roll of first-class postage stamps.
3. Read all the refund offers in *Dollars Daily* carefully. Mark the ones that interest you with a yellow crayon or felt-tipped marker.
4. Check your label collection and cabinets to see if you have the labels needed for the refund. If you can use the product, put it on your shopping list. Try to plan menus around refundable products.
5. If you have the labels and the form, clip them together and mail immediately to the correct address. If you don't have the form, and the offer does not specifically ask for it, try without the

form. Companies usually pay anyway. Using a plain piece of paper, print your name, address, and ZIP code clearly, and request the refund.

6. Mail your refund request before the expiration date. Once the date is past, the offer is void.

7. Wait for your refund to arrive. It seems like an eternity for that first refund to be delivered. Most refunds take from four to six weeks, but some have taken up to three months. So be patient; companies always send what they promise.

8. While waiting for your refunds, continue sending for more. If you mail one every day, in a few weeks you should receive dollars daily.

9. Put your refunding money in a piggy bank or savings account to save for something special. That's how our family can afford a vacation every year.

10. When refunding, make sure you read *all* the information carefully and send *exactly* what the company has requested. All offers are usually good throughout the United States unless otherwise stated.

REFUNDING WORK SHEET

1. Did you have the refund form or mail-in certificate from a newspaper, magazine, or store?

                              Yes_____ No_____

Remember, try sending refund requests on plain paper if the actual refund form is not available. You must use the correct address and send the specific qualifiers requested. Keep a list of companies that pay without forms and another list of those that refuse payment unless the required certificate is included with the request.

2. Did you enclose the correct qualifiers?

YES_____ No_____

Send exactly what is requested. It may be the Proof of Purchase seal, UPC (Universal Product Code), ingredient panel, box top or bottom, net weight, or entire label. An accompanying cash register tape or favorite brand label such as a bread wrapper is sent only when requested on the form. If you are in doubt, check the wording on the form and package and make an educated guess. The worst thing that could happen is that you will receive your incorrect qualifiers back with a more detailed explanation. Some forms are difficult to decipher, and occasionally even I have to guess which proof of purchase is desired. Sometimes the refund form is not exactly clear. Usually the qualifier is spelled out simply, and once you get into the swing of refunding, it becomes a snap.

3. Did you address the envelope correctly?

Yes_____ No_____

Do not use the manufacturer's address on the packaging. They usually do not handle refund promotions but will employ a clearinghouse or specify a particular box number.

4. Did you clearly print your name, address, and ZIP code on your request?

Yes_____ No_____

Remember that name-and-address stickers are efficient and ensure accuracy. It is a good idea to place these on the envelopes when stamping them and to keep the whole box of envelopes ready for mailing with stamps and return addresses.

5. Did you stamp the envelope?

Yes____ No____

No sense cluttering the Dead Letter Office. This is the most common error of new refunders who are puzzled as to why they did not receive their refund as promised. If your return address is on the envelope, you may receive it back marked "returned for postage." If you have also forgotten the return address, it is a problem.

6. Did you make a record of your refund request?

Yes____ No____

You may decide to use one of my record keeping models or devise your own. If you don't keep any records, you will never know how profitable your hobby has become. (Samples will follow.)

Set Up a Space for Refunding

Set aside a small area for your refunding. Some people like to work in front of the television set so that they can watch their favorite soap opera and earn money at the same time.

I can tell you from personal experience that the kitchen table has its limitations as a work site since mealtime means relocation. A desk is ideal, because you can keep everything handy with a minimum of shuffling forms, envelopes, and papers. Cellophane tape, scissors, marking pens, staples, and a stapler are all tools of the trade. When you become organized, you can spare more time for your main pursuit, getting a return on your grocery bill. I prefer keeping my refunding tools in a shoe box placed in the right-hand drawer of my king-sized desk, where they can be reached quickly. However, I started my refunding hobby on the kitchen table and well remember the trials and tribulations of dinnertime approaching while I was still engulfed in labels. Jim finally grew weary of late dinners and constant complaints of gravy stains on refund forms, so he built a massive desk to my refunding specifications. "Make plenty of room on top," I instructed, "and a large drawer on the right-hand side to hold partial deals, labels, letters from pen pals, and my refunding record files."

Partial deals are not quite ready to be mailed but may require a missing link. For example, the refund may call for two soup box tops and a bread wrapper. If I have the soup tops handy, I will staple them to the refund form and place this partial deal in a holding file until I locate the bread wrapper.

Everyone can find enough space for refunding. In my mobile home every inch was accounted for, so I became superorganized. Some subscribers are fortunate enough to have a dream house with a whole room reserved for refunding! People have sewing rooms, dens, and studies, but the refunding room pays its own rent.

Keep a small box in the kitchen to save labels and wrappers from everyday meals. Soap, detergent or cereal boxes that will later become qualifiers are perfect. When the small box becomes filled to the brim, you should place the labels into a larger carton for future filing. Eventually you must file efficiently in order to locate proofs of purchase when required. Disorganized clutter will eventually land in the wastebasket, and refunding dollars will go down the drain. Do not delay in setting up a filing system before you become discouraged. (There will be more about easy filing systems in the next chapter.)

Set a Goal

Be realistic. Don't expect too much too soon. Refunds may take more than six weeks to arrive, but remember that they are not gimmicks and always pay as advertised. Consider the gigantic advertising budget needed for one moment of prime-time television, and then there is no guarantee that the consumer will even try the product. Manufacturers offer refunds to introduce you to new products and reacquaint you with old favorites. When I was a little girl, I used to badger Mom, "Why don't they invent new food? I'm tired of the old food." Today's supermarket shelves are stocked with new products guaranteed to add spice and variety to menus. Without refunding I couldn't afford to try these extra-special creations and wouldn't be aware of their existence if I didn't scout refunding opportunities.

Remember, profits depend upon how much time and effort are put into your new hobby and upon your family's cooperation. If they are willing to try new brands, you may participate in more offers.

Switch Brands

I am not a coffee drinker, but when a coupon for a free jar arrived in the mail, I tried it. I discovered one brand of coffee that I could really enjoy without an aftertaste. I am not usually faithful to one particular brand or supermarket since my shopping revolves around refunding possibilities. Not all brands are carried by any one grocery chain, so I stop and shop until I have located featured refundable products. However, we all have our favorites when it comes to coffee, tea, and cigarettes. Even if you refuse to switch brands, you will still receive refunds if you favor national brand items. If you prefer a particular brand of pancake mix or syrup, use it, but save the label on speculation for future money-making possibilities. Aunt Jemima®, an old-time favorite of our family, had a multitude of offers recently. Some called for specific items like frozen waffles, but others gave a mix-and-match opportunity to clear out the label file and stock up for the future.

In refunding, you learn as you earn. Refunding is more than a national pastime; it has become a way of life for the vast network of refunders throughout the entire country.

Now suppose you need something for which you do not have a coupon. If you want to bake a devil's food cake and don't have a coupon for chocolate frosting, check stores, newspapers or *Dollars Daily* to see which brand currently offers a refund. Purchase that particular product, and immediately send the required qualifier (box top, bottom, universal code, net weight, proof of purchase seal, ingredient statement, or what-

Can you resist trying a new product when you will receive another absolutely free? Many of these innovations are fantastic, like the Success® Rice that cooks in its own plastic wrap, or the cake roll that freezes until sudden company arrives and then becomes bake-shop fresh.

ever is specified) for a refund. If there isn't a current offer available at that time, purchase a favorite national brand of icing that has previously offered refunds, and file the label for future opportunities. It doesn't matter if you prefer a prepared cake mix as I do, or are a more sophisticated baker who bakes from scratch. All major companies offer refunds. Flour, sugar, eggs, chocolate chips, nuts, and milk are all refundable items.

Every year millions of dollars in refunds remain unclaimed by unknowledgeable customers. Be aware, and claim your fair share of coupons and cash-backs. Remember, a refund a day chases inflation blues away.

Plan Carefully

Refunding is like a game of Scrabble®: you can juggle your letters for maximum points. Consider all possibilities of each individual offer before action. In the case illustrated below, you could send three empty packages of Kool Super Lights® for a silver dollar or two end flaps and two empty packs for two silver dollars. The offer was limited to one per family or address. However, if you purchased one carton, you certainly could send for your two dollars and still be able to send a silver dollar to each of your two best friends.

There are many current cigarette offers that still hold these possibilities. I am not encouraging you to smoke, but if you must, save your empties and cash in on that terrible habit.

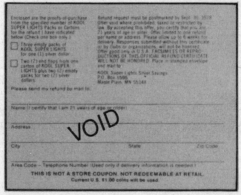

Deadlines

Keep deadlines in mind since they are final. Don't wait until the end of the last stretch with a minute to go. Send for refunds early. Don't expect to win the refunding race in record time or set a track record. Smart refunders start slowly but always have a strong finish. Don't quit in the stretch while time lags between mailing date and actual receipt of your refund bonus. Continue to enter refund races until you receive a refund every day.

Set Up Record Keeping

Some refunders like to keep accurate records of all refunds. Personally I don't keep extensive records because I'd rather spend that valuable time mailing more refunds and stick to my five-hour-a-week refunding schedule. I do keep simple records of how much cash and coupons arrive, placing the money in a separate bank account for our family vacations. It is easy for dollars to trickle through our fingers, and without any record whatsoever, you will never have any idea of your profits.

If you desire to keep a detailed list of every refund requested, you may set up a system in a notebook similar to this example. This will also indicate which companies usually pay without forms in addition to the amount received.

EXPLANATION OF RECORD KEEPING CHART
1. Enter the name of the refund.
2. List the address, including box number, where you are mailing the refund. Keep in mind that a different box number *usually* denotes a separate offer, so you may safely mail away for both without violating the one-to-a-customer rule.
3. Fill in the amount if it is cash. If it is a free coupon, list the product name and approximate value of the coupon. When sending for free premium gifts, mark the estimated value if it is not given on the form.

RECORD KEEPING CHART

1 Name of Refund	2 Address	3 Value of Refund	4 Form Sent (Yes or No)	5 Date Mailed	6 Date Received	& 7 Outstanding
Ragú®	Box NB 102	$2.00 coupons	No	1-2	2-4	
Ragú®	Box NB 152	Free jar (approx. $.89)	Yes	1-2	2-1	
Lux®	Box 724A	$1.00	Yes	1-2	2-8	
R. T. French®	Box 22699	Corning Ware cookware $4.49 value	No	1-2		√
Sun Lite®	Box 9695	$2.00	Yes	1-5	2-7	
Underwood®	Box NB 374	$1.00	No	1-10		√
Green Giant®	Box 107	$1.00	No	1-10	Refused	
Dow	Box 5555	$4.00	Yes	1-5	2-7	
Total received for one week		$9.89				

(Note: Green Giant® has been crossed off the list, indicating a refusal notice was received since that company requires a refund form to accompany each request.)

4. If you used a form, mark "yes." If not, indicate "no." When you send for a refund without a form and receive a refusal notice, draw a line through the entry and mark "refused" in the "date received" column. This will be a terrific refunding aid when sending future refunds, and after a while you may be able to anticipate which companies require forms. You should keep a separate list of these companies for future reference. Many refunders favor manufacturers who generously pay without refund forms.

5. When sending your refund, fill in the date mailed. Remember, refunds take from four to six weeks to arrive. Some have taken four months, so please be patient. Don't send the company or clearinghouse reminder notices after the six-week period has lapsed. After three months, if you still have an outstanding refund, it may help to write to the company itself, not the clearinghouse. You can find the manufacturer's address on the product packaging. Sometimes clearinghouses get backlogged, and writing to them will cause only a greater delay and add to their problems of efficiently expediting refund requests. Refunds are generally mailed bulk rate as a postage economy measure, so your refund may be slow.

6. When you receive your refund, fill in the date.

7. In order to figure your monthly total, add the total amount of cash and free coupons received. Check the "date received" column, and add the total value received during the month. Open space in the column indicates an outstanding refund. Checkmark outstanding refunds in the last column so that you can indicate receipt later. When the refund finally arrives, cross out the check mark, and fill in the date

received. You may wish to keep three separate totals: (1) the amount of cash returns; (2) the coupon value received; and (3) a list of premium gifts.

You may decide on a complex refund bookkeeping system or the quick-and-easy record that I prefer. Perhaps you would like to try various systems until you discover one that best suits your needs. I simply list all free gifts received and make a daily note of cash received and coupon values. The cash is deposited weekly into my refunding vacation savings account with deductions only for refunding expenses.

Some refunders also deposit the cash value of each coupon redeemed since this represents money they would have spent for groceries if the free coupons were not available. Your savings account will grow more rapidly this way.

I like the *quick-and-easy refund record* because I can tell at a glance exactly how much money I have saved by refunding for cash and coupons. When I look at my vacation savings account, I know just how much cash I have received free and clear.

EXAMPLE: QUICK-AND-EASY REFUND RECORD

Monday	Tuesday	Wednesday	Thursday	Friday	Saturday	Weekly Total
$1.00	$ .50	$2.50	$ .75	$1.00	$4.50	$10.25
2.00	1.00	1.75	2.50	3.00	1.50	11.75
4.00	1.00	3.00	2.00	.50	4.00	14.50
2.00	.50	3.50	6.00	.50	.50	13.00
	Monthly Total					49.50
1.00	.75	2.50	4.00	.50	1.25	10.00
2.00	1.25	3.00	2.00	2.25	1.75	12.25
1.50	4.50	1.00	4.00	3.00	1.00	15.00
3.00	1.00	1.00	2.50	4.00	7.25	18.75
	Monthly Total					56.00
	Total for Two Months					105.50

FREE GIFTS RECEIVED DURING THE MONTH OF JANUARY

Gift	Approximate value
Cigarette Lighter (Carlton 100's®)	$1.25
Hand Puppet (Ice pops)	2.00
Vegetable Steamer (Dulany®)	?
Yo-Yo (Kellogg's®)	1.00
Tony the Tiger Pen (Kellogg's®)	?
Plastic Feeder Water Dish (Kleen Kitty®)	4.00
Stainless Steel Knife (Frozen dinner)	4.95
1,000 Name-and-Address Labels (Waldorf®)	2.00

Place the name of the company in parentheses so that you will know where the premium came from, and list the approximate retail price, if known.

Supplies Checklist

Envelopes ☐
Stamps ☐
Pens ☐
Scrap paper ☐
Scissors ☐
Paper clips ☐
Stapler ☐
Staples ☐
Cellophane tape ☐
Address stickers or rubber stamp
with your name and address ☐
Glue or paste ☐

The best things in life are free.

I suggest starting with a package of one hundred small envelopes (approximately three by six inches) and a roll of first-class postage stamps. The last nonrefundable bargain in the world is a stamp-roll holder on sale at your local post office for a nickel. In order to be time efficient and superorganized, you must make each motion count. I usually paste all stamps on envelopes in a few minutes' sitting while keeping up to date on soap operas. This eliminates the error of forgetting to stamp envelopes when mailing each individual refund.

Your return address on the envelope is very important, for if the box is closed, you forget to stamp your letter, or anything else goes wrong, you will automatically receive your qualifiers and form back. The Post Office will no longer deliver letters without postage but instead may send you the following notice with a forty-cent charge. You then have to remail the request with postage and have lost valuable time in addition to added cost.

UNITED STATES POST OFFICE
Philadelphia, Pa. 19104
Dead Letter Office

Date: Feb 6, 1979

This letter had to be opened in the Dead Letter Office to determine the return address. The fee for this service is 40 cents. If your return address had been on the envelope, this letter would have been returned to you free of charge. If your return address was not on the inside, this letter would have been disposed of.

Please get in the habit of putting your return address on all your mail. If your letter cannot be delivered, at least you will know the reason.

Thank you.

Superintendent

You may wish to begin refunding with a smaller investment for postage and to use refunds as received for additional stamps. If you already stamped the envelope and then make an error in addressing that cannot be corrected, you can lift the stamp from the envelope and reapply it to another envelope with glue. Or you may cover the error with plain paper and readdress correctly. Remember to use the address on the refund form or in *Dollar Daily*, not the manufacturer's address on the product itself.

Expenses

I don't keep an expense record, because any cash spent for postage, envelopes, or other supplies comes out of my refunding bank account.

Whenever you see envelopes on sale (or any other refunding needs), purchase a huge supply and store them for future use. In the long run, it is worthwhile to squirrel away refunding supplies to prevent running out to the store in the midst of the end-of-the-month crush when you are trying to beat deadlines with postmarks. I don't believe in a monthly expense chart since I suggest stocking up and buying ahead. However, you can keep an annual record, by using the following simple guide.

ANNUAL REFUNDING EXPENSES

Date	Purchases	Quantity	Cost
Jan. 2	*Dollars Daily* refunding newspaper	12 issues	$ 7.50
Jan. 4	Pens	3	1.00
Jan. 4	Envelopes (100 to a package)	10 pkgs.	5.90
Jan. 7	First-class postage stamps	100	15.00
Feb. 4	*Coupon Queen Special* (Round-up of current refund offers)	1 issue	1.50

6

How to Make the Most of Labels

What to Save and How to File

My general refunding rule is: *Save Everything!* However, collections can get out of control, so in order to be practical and space-efficient, I will list the bare minimum of essentials for any good label collection.

Save every label you use. When you purchase a product, you pay for the packaging as well as the contents, which both belong to you. All national brand labels, boxes, and wrappers have value. Sometimes your local supermarket will offer a store-brand item for a penny. Naturally, you never refuse a bargain. Refunders save store-brand labels for use when manufacturers request your favorite product label to accompany the main refund request.

Whenever you decide not to save entire wrappings, you risk the possibility of discarding the refundable portion. Companies are notorious for changing qualifiers, but from my previous experience, I recom-

DU PONT
RAIN DANCE
CAR WAX

$1.00 BACK
from Du Pont,
with proof of purchase
offer expires Dec. 31, 1981
(details inside)

VOID

Keeps on Beading and Shining
Rain after Rain, Wash after Wash.
Guaranteed

WARNING!
CAUSES EYE IRRITATION.
COMBUSTIBLE See Back Panel

16 FL.OZ.(1PT.)
473ml

LEE air filter
AFLA

VOID

COLOR CODED BY MAKE OF CAR

HOW TO SEND FOR YOUR CASH REBATE

1. Cut out "THE LEE ELIMINATORS" from top of this air filter package and send along with receipt or back register tape that shows you purchased a LEE air filter. Please circle price you paid.

2. Print name of purchase plus your NAME, ADDRESS, CITY, STATE, ZIP for LEE FILTER REBATE, P.O. Box 17421, Cleveland, Ohio 44117

3. Limit of one $1.00 cash rebate per envelope.

4. Offer good only in U.S.A. and void where prohibited or otherwise restricted.

5. Allow 4-6 weeks for cash rebate.

FREE PRIME GAS DRYER
WITH PROOF OF PURCHASE
FROM "PRIME" GAS DRYER, PLUS
ONE OF THE PRODUCTS SHOWN
HERE

Your purchase price
refunded by mail
up to $1.00

*IMPORTANT, see back for details.

Mail to: "PRIME" Gas Dryer Cash Refund
P.O. Box 4504, Chicago, Ill. 60677

VOID

Name _____
Address _____
City _____ State _____ Zip _____

"PRIME" Gas Dryer Cash Refund

mail on _____
date

Please allow 4 to 6 weeks for refund.
LIMIT ONE REFUND PER FAMILY

TAKE ONE

KEEP YOUR GUARD UP

Free Spot Lite
12 VOLT PLUG-IN

when you buy 2
gallons of Dowgard

Dowgard

VOID

SEE DETAILS ON REVERSE SIDE

Many a man's best friend is his car, and a woman's, too! Treat your car to refundable products, and it will gleam inside and out. Automotive product refunds are everyday offers.

60¢ BACK
(includes postage)

on *Rally* Cream Wax

(8 ounce size only)

SEE DETAILS ON BACK

E-11764

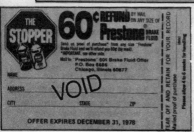

THE STOPPER

60¢ REFUND BY MAIL
ON ANY SIZE OF

Prestone BRAKE FLUID

Send us proof of purchase from any size "Prestone" Brake Fluid and we'll refund you 60¢ by mail. *IMPORTANT, see other side.

Mail to: Prestone 60¢ Brake Fluid Offer
P.O. Box 6686
Chicago, Illinois 60677

NAME

ADDRESS

CITY   STATE   ZIP

OFFER EXPIRES DECEMBER 31, 1978

TEAR OFF AND RETAIN FOR YOUR RECORD
Mailed proof of purchase
Please allow 4 to 6 weeks for handling

GAS MI$ER
BUY ONE... GET ONE FREE!
WITH PROOF OF PURCHASE OF "GAS MISER"
Your purchase price refunded by mail up to $1.00

OFFER EXPIRES DEC. 31, 1978.
See reverse side for details.

AS-3064G

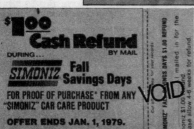

$1⁰⁰ Cash Refund
BY MAIL

DURING...

SIMONIZ Fall Savings Days

FOR PROOF OF PURCHASE* FROM ANY "SIMONIZ" CAR CARE PRODUCT

OFFER ENDS JAN. 1, 1979.

*See reverse side for details.

AS-3062C

"SIMONIZ" FALL SAVINGS DAYS $1.00 REFUND

On Simoniz $1.00 Refund, mailed in for the
Please allow 4-6 weeks for refund

mend that the following be utilized as a basic list of items to save.

With *Boxed Products* slit the box down the seams. Discard any portion of the box that does not have writing on it. Next flatten the box so that it does not take much space. After awhile you will master the skill of peeling boxes. With your fingernails, you can separate excess cardboard from the back of the label to make it slim and compact. This is not only a space saver but also gives you lower postal rates when mailing.

To remove labels from *Canned Goods*, take a knife and run it along the seam of the label, and it will slip off easily. When removing the label before using contents, be sure to use a felt-tipped marker to identify what is inside the can.

When saving the containers of *Car Products*, make a note of the code number from the bottom of the can and the price paid. On Prestone® products, record the AS-number, which is usually located on the back of the can.

Note *Code Numbers* from various aerosol products that do not have paper labels, such as hair spray, deodorants, spray disinfectants, and furniture polish. It is a good idea to use three-by-five-inch index cards in a small file so that you may easily refer to them.

Remove the tops of *Glass Jars and Bottles*. If they contain a small paper or plastic inner liner, save these before discarding tops. Soak the bottle or jar in hot water. If the label on the plastic bottle stubbornly refuses to soak off, cut the plastic around the label with a heated knife. Usually, if you run the knife under running hot water from the tap, it will help. Joy,® Downy,® and Palmolive® dishwashing liquid labels are the most difficult to remove. Yet it is worth the effort because they all have frequent refunds. It is easier to cut the plastic than battle the seemingly iron glue. After removing the label, be sure to place it on waxed paper, plastic wrap, or paper toweling to dry. *Never* place soaked labels face down or they will adhere to your counter top or table.

Net Weights: When saving the bottom of a box, tear upward from the bottom of the box, leaving the net weight attached so that if required, it will be easily identifiable.

When opening packages, never discard *tearstrips*.

It is a good idea to save all *Universal Product Codes* (UPC) symbols. Always mark the product name and size on back.

BABY PRODUCTS

Baby cereal: Save the tops and bottoms with the net weight statements attached.

Baby food: Save entire labels.

Disposal diapers: Save UPC symbols and front panels. (Pampers® previously required the size ovals but now wants the words "Disposable Diapers.")

BEVERAGES

Frozen juices: Save the white plastic tear strips.

Minute Maid® orange juice: Save the words, "Fresh if used by the above date" from cartons.

Powdered and canned drinks: Kool-Aid®, Funny Face®, Country Time®, Minute Maid®, Hi-C®, Hawaiian Punch®—Save the entire label or envelope.

Soda: With six-packs, save the proof of purchase

seal or the plastic carrier holding the cans together. Canada Dry® sometimes wants neckbands. Save all plastic liners from bottled soda tops. Mark the back of each for identification. Pry the plastic liners (found inside the metal caps) out with a knife. Never mail the metal caps.

BOXED GOODS

Dried milk: Save front, tops, bottoms with net weight statement attached, nutrition panel, and proof of purchase seals.

Jell-O®: Save front panel.

Nestlé Quik®: Save proof of purchase seal.

Pancake mix: Save proof of purchase seal and ingredient panel.

Rice: Save proof of purchase seal, tops, and bottoms with net weight.

Royal® puddings and gelatin: Save front panel.

Stuffing mixes: Save proof of purchase seal, top and bottom panels with net weight, and inner envelopes.

Shake n' Bake®: Save inner envelopes and entire box.

BREAD WRAPPERS

Save a few bread wrappers of any brand. Sometimes offers for other products require an accompanying bread wrapper from your favorite brand.

BUTTER

Land O'Lakes®: known to switch qualifiers. They currently require proof of purchase seals.

CAKE MIXES

Save entire front panel, including net weight, tops, and bottom of boxes.

CANDY

Save entire cellophane bag, ingredient panel from six-pack packages, individual bar and entire wrappings.

CANNED PRODUCTS

Fruit, vegetable, juices, Chinese food, milk, pudding, tuna fish, and more. Save entire labels.

CAT FOOD

Save entire can labels. Boxed cat food may require proof of purchase seals, tops, or bottoms with net weight statements.

CEREAL

Save box tops and bottoms and proof of purchase seal, if there is one. General Mills® usually requests box bottoms.

CHEESE

Save entire wrappers.

CLOTHING

Save pantyhose and undergarment wrappers and sales slips.

CIGARETTES

Save entire packages. Discard cellophane and inner foil. Flatten packs. Be sure to save the closure seals. Save the end flaps of cartons.

CLEANING PRODUCTS

Save entire labels, front and back. Cut labels away from plastic bottles such as dishwashing detergents, fabric softeners, and liquid washing detergents when they fail to soak away easily.

Ajax® and *Comet®* cleansers: Cut away net weight.

Dow® bathroom cleaner: Save plastic top.

COFFEE

Save plastic lids, but trim away edges so that they will be flat. Also keep a record of code numbers from the bottom of the can for your card file.

Instant coffee: Save inner seals and labels.

COOKIES AND CRACKERS

Save all proof of purchase seals.

DETERGENT BOXES

Tops and bottoms with net weight designations.

When removing bottoms of detergent boxes, tear upward so that the net weight statement remains attached for easy identification.

DOG FOOD

Save entire can labels. Save boxed food tops, bottoms with net weight, proof of purchase seal, ingredient panels.

Bagged dog food: Save net weight circles.

Gaines®: Always save the portion of the box with the starred price mark.

Starred price spot from boxed product.

DRUG DEPARTMENT ITEMS

Save entire cartons from aspirins, cough syrups, toothpaste, deodorants, bath oil, cotton balls, Q-tips®, personal products, razors and more.

Band-Aids®: Save all individual wrappers. If they come in a cardboard box save that also.

EGG CARTONS

Save a few tops with price mark. Trim away edges to store flat.

ELECTRIC

Small and major appliance receipts, ownership and warranty cards and instruction manuals. Light bulbs—save outer package.

FLOUR

Save bottom flap and net weight.

FROSTINGS

Save entire can labels. On boxed frosting, save the box top and the bottom with net weight.

FROZEN FOODS

Flatten and save entire boxes from all products of major brands (seafood, meats, vegetables, rice, macaroni, etc.). If you really must condense space, discard the back panels but keep the UPC, ingredient panel, directions, and nutritional information panel.

GRAVY

Save the entire envelope or label.

GUM

Save individual and outer wrappers.

JELLIES AND JAMS

Save front and back labels.

KETCHUP

Save neckbands, front, and back labels.

MARGARINE

Save all cartons from name brands.

MAYONNAISE

Save front and back labels.

MEAT

Save stickers from packages of chopped meat, steak, poultry, ham, chops, etc. Also, save all chicken and turkey tags. Trim away turkey wrappers saving all printed portions.

Bacon: With any brand, save entire packaging.
Cold cuts: Save entire wrappers.
Frozen meat products: Save entire boxes.
Hot dogs, or other processed meats: front wrappers.

MILK PRODUCTS
Cremora® or dried milk: Save inner seals and entire labels.
Boxed products: Save tops and bottoms with net weight statements.
Ice cream: Save a few entire cartons of any brand.
Sour cream: Save lids.
Yogurt: Save lids.

MISCELLANEOUS
Cricket® lighters: Save entire blister card.
Batteries: Eveready® or Ray-O-Vac®: Save entire cards. Discard cellophane without print.

MOUTHWASH
Cepacol®: Save red shoulder sticker.
Lavoris®: Save front and back labels.
Listerine®: Save front and back label, also entire outer wrapper.
Listermint®: Save entire label.
Scope®: Save front and back labels.
Signal®: Save front and back labels.

PAPER PRODUCTS
Napkins: Save entire packaging.

>   *Tissues:* Kleenex®. Save proof of purchase seal, UPC, and open tear strips.
>   *Marcal®*: Save UPC quality seal, and open tear strips.
>   *Toilet paper:* Save entire wrappers. Trim away cellophane without print.
>   *Towels:* Save entire wrappers. Trim away cellophane without print.

PEANUT BUTTER

Save front and back labels.

PIE CRUST

Save proof of purchase seals and tops and bottoms.
Johnston's®: Entire label.

PLASTIC WRAP AND BAGS

>   *Baggies®*: Now wants the words "Colgate-Palmolive Company." Previously called for end panel with the red star.
>   *Glad®*: Save UPC and tear strips. In the past they have also requested proof of purchase seals, end panels, etc.
>   *Handi-Wrap®*: Save arrow tear strip.
>   *Hefty®*: Save proof of purchase seals.
>   *Kordite®*: Save proof of purchase seals.
>   *Saran Wrap®*: Save arrow tear strips.
>   *Ziploc®*: Save perforated opening tab strip.

SALAD DRESSINGS

Save front and back labels, neckbands, and inner seals.

SHAMPOO

Save front and back labels and inner seals.

SNACKS

Borden Devil Dogs,®, Yodels®, etc. Save proof of purchase seals and ingredient panels.

Hunt's®, Del Monte® Snack Pak: Save entire cardboard packaging from four-can wrapping.
Potato chips, cheese snacks, etc.: Save entire bags.
Pretzels: Save proof of purchase seals.
Pringles®: Save outside wrappers.

SPAGHETTI SAUCE

Save entire jar or can labels.

SPICES

Adolph's®, Lawry's®, etc.: Save entire labels.
Barbecue sauce: Save front and back label and neckband.

SUGAR AND SUGAR SUBSTITUTES

Save entire bottle labels. On boxes save proof of purchase seals, tops and bottoms.

SYRUP

Save front and back labels, neckbands, and cap liners.

TEA

Save inner seals and labels from instant tea, the entire front panel with net weight from boxes, and cellophane bags from envelopes of instant tea.

TOYS

With national brands such as Kenner®, save proof of purchase seals.

Filing Systems

Organize your labels and qualifiers early in the game so that you will remain totally in charge before labels control you. Start with an empty carton and manilla folders marked into categories. Some refunders prefer large brown grocery bags cut down in height or clear plastic bags. Be sure to flatten all labels and boxes. Try peeling cardboard backing away so that bulky boxes will be paper thin. Beginners should save entire packaging until they are knowledgeable about correct qualifiers. This section listing refundable portions to save in limited space will be of assistance. However, only practice in mailing refunds will prove whether you fully understand which are refundable portions. Remember, the Universal Product Code is not always the proof of purchase. Do not snip all U.P.C. numbers from packages, jumble them together in an envelope, and expect to receive a return. Once you have changed from beginner to pro, you may slim your collections and take the risk of losing occasional refunds as I did when Pampers® changed qualifiers. I save only proof of purchase seals on snack crackers, cookies, dog biscuits, and dry cat food. Some day I'll be sorry. However, you have to draw the line somewhere, and only trial and error will tell what is best. Become completely familiar with refund requirements before you venture on an impulsive clean-up campaign only to discover you have discarded the refunds and saved nonrefundable portions.

Vary product categories to meet the needs of your family's shopping list. Naturally, if you have teenagers, you won't need a baby food folder (unless one of them decides to become a teenaged bride as I did). If you don't have a pet, you won't need a folder for pet food. However, besides offering companionship a family pet will provide you with many opportunities for refunds on cat and dog food. I'm a true animal lover and own a cat and a dog.

MARY ANNE'S FILING SYSTEM

Baby Products (Baby food, juices, cereal, disposable diapers, etc.)

Bakery Products (Bread, frozen cakes, packaged cake and cookies, flour, pie crust, etc.)

Beverages (Soda, coffee, tea, etc.)

Butter (Margarine)

Candy (Gum)

Cereal (Hot and cold)

Cheese (Hard, soft, soft cheese spread)

Chinese Food (Soy sauce, chow mein noodles, chop suey, egg rolls, canned and frozen vegetables)

Clothing (Panty hose, undergarments, etc.)

Detergents (Soaps, bleach, dishwashing liquids, laundry soap powder, floor wax, etc.)

Drug Store Items (Personal products, cosmetics, aspirin, cough syrup, etc.)

Eggs

Electrical Appliances (light bulbs, small and major appliances)

Frozen Foods (pot pies, casseroles, etc.)

Fruit (Fresh, canned, frozen and dried fruits)

Gelatin

Ice Cream

Juice (Canned and frozen juice drinks)

Macaroni (Canned, boxed; spaghetti and other noodle or pasta products)

Meat (Fresh and frozen)

Miscellaneous (Cash register tape, lighters, batteries, charcoal, toys, school supplies)

Milk (Fresh, canned, powdered, coffee creamer, etc.)

Paper Products (Paper towels, tissues, toilet tissue, napkins, paper cups, etc.)

Pet Food (Cat and dog food, kitty litter)

Pizza (Frozen and boxed)

Potatoes (Canned and frozen)

Pudding (Canned and boxed)

Rice (All rice products)

Sauce (Spaghetti Sauce, Ketchup, Salad Dressing, etc.)

Seafood (Tuna fish, canned and frozen seafood products)

Seasonings (Salt, spices, meat tenderizer, etc.)

Shampoo (Hair spray, creme rinse, conditioners, hair color)

Snacks (Potato chips, pretzels, pop corn, etc.)

Soup (Canned and boxed soups)

Sugar (Sugar substitutes)

Tobacco (Cigarettes, cigars, etc.)

Toothpaste (Toothbrushes)

Vegetables (Canned, bottled, and frozen)

You may use this list as a general guide, but feel free to modify it, inventing categories to suit your individual needs. Be sure to schedule enough time for filing. A clumsy bag of loose, disorganized boxes can turn into a file when properly trimmed, peeled, and flattened. Organize your filing system, and try to file at least once a week to keep labels at your fingertips when needed.

I lived in a mobile home and still had plenty of room

for my label collection. Out of necessity I learned to compact my refunding and become superorganized. Some refunders develop their own systems of filing, preferring to keep qualifiers by product name rather than type of product. Their folders may indicate Green Giant®, Del Monte®, Hunt's®, Libby®, for example, instead of product categories as mine does. This system has its advantages: If a refund calls for ten Del Monte® labels, you can locate them all in one folder, whereas I would find it necessary to look up fruit, juice, vegetables, tomato sauce, ketchup, etc. However, I created my own filing system and find it comfortable and easy to manage.

When saving inner seals, soda-cap liners, UPC, or proof of purchase seals, be sure to mark the back of each qualifier so that it may be easily identifiable. Companies frequently change packaging, but they always honor old labels. I have never been refused a refund because the label was outdated. Once my kitchen sink overflowed and the carton of labels stuffed beneath the sink drain was dripping wet. I thought the entire collection was ruined and lost forever but refused to part with potential money makers. The entire day was spent drying soaked and battered labels that eventually brought cash back.

Small qualifiers such as proof of purchase seals may be easily lost in the main file, so I place them in a small plastic bag first.

It is a convenient time saver to keep a small card file with frequently requested product code numbers recorded.

Cash register tapes are filed in my "Miscellaneous" folder. Since the tape may be required for more than one offer, I merely cut off the section with the correct amount on it, circle the price, and mark the product name on the tape next to the appropriate amount. Some supermarkets have an accurate electronic computer readout of each tape as the Universal Product Code is passed over the scanner. The name and product size are printed along with the prices, simplifying check-out procedures at the store and acting as a refunding aid later.

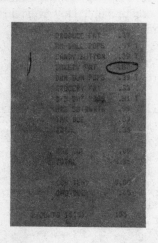
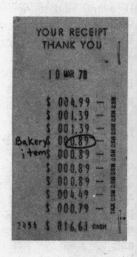

If you are not fortunate enough to have an electronic read-out like the tape on the left, just use your cash receipt, circle the correct amount, and write the name of the item next to it, as we've done with the tape on the right. Most companies (not Max Factor) will accept a portion of the tape, so you may save the rest for other refunds. However, if you know you will need the receipt for a special refund, ask the clerk at the check-out counter to ring the item separately.

When in Doubt, Don't Throw it Out! It is usually safe to keep only proof of purchase seals on Kordite® and Hefty® plastic bags, but they may change their qualifier policy at any time. Glad® is notorious for switching qualifiers, which may result in several refunds received for the same package if you were wise enough to save it all. Although they print a proof of purchase seal, they rarely call for it. They usually ask for the UPC number, but I have collected on Glad®end panels, proof of purchase seals, UPC numbers, special coins printed on some packages, specially marked packages with coupons for one free, and the words "2 Ply." Companies have changed required qualifiers from ingredient panels to package fronts; from box tops to inner foil envelopes. You never can tell what they will ask for, so be prepared. It's like the old-time auctions Nana tells me about. Between double features, the theater would have an auction and buy certain items from the audience for fun (as Monty Hall occasionally does during the last few minutes on some "Let's Make a Deal" television shows). The family would attend the fun shows with a shopping bag full of surprises ready for the emcee's request. Once Mom was nibbling on an apple when he called for an apple core, and she won the prize. Another time Nana hobbled home minus her left shoe after Grandpa Andy raced up to the stage when a women's left shoe was requested for a cash rebate.

You will pick up filing shortcuts as you go along, but the main idea is to organize a system early in the game and continue to keep qualifiers in some sort of order. Misplaced labels are valueless when a refund rolls around. It can be especially frustrating when you know you have the qualifier but simply can't locate it. Proper filing routinely accomplished can turn disorganized chaos into a smooth operation.

Part of the *fun* of re*fun*ding is trying to outfox the manufacturers *legally*. Use the products but save the packaging so you will be shipshape and able to race for the refund as soon as it is announced.

7

How to Beat the System

Combat That One-to-a-Customer Rule

Many refunders ask how to combat the one-to-a-customer rule. This depends upon what you consider a family to be. My own interpretation is "one to a family at an address or household." Therefore I would utilize extra, complete deals (qualifier and refund form) for Nana or Mom to show them I am thinking of them. They live in different residences, do not share the same family units, provide for their own households, and simply don't have the time or the inclination to refund for themselves, so I can see no violation of rules. In return, Nana and Mom might save their extra labels for me. I use whatever I wish for myself and alternate sending duplicates to either of them.

Now remember, different box numbers or a change in expiration date or qualifiers often indicate totally different offers. But not always, so read forms carefully. One company may have several offers running simultaneously for the same product. They may all be for different amounts of cash or vary in merchandise premiums. If expiration dates, etc. were different, and I had the labels, I would send to each new offer available.

Other refunders devise dubious methods of receiving duplicate refunds for the same product. I dare not vouch for their legality or sanction their methods. They prefer one particular brand and do not wish to switch brands as I eagerly do. They feel entitled to several refunds since they actually use the product many times.

Now if you happen to send a dozen identical requests in the same handwriting with special stationery to the same address, I am certain someone would spot this extraordinary attempt to receive a multitude of duplicate refunds. Certainly, if I were the employee assigned to the promotion, I would be suspicious. That's one of the reasons I had to resort to the required coupon that must accompany subscribers' requests addressed to *Dollars Daily* Free Form Club. I wanted to share extra refund forms sent by subscribers who were lucky enough to locate them but unable to take advantage of all offers. However, after a while I repeatedly noticed the same color of ink and fancy stationery or the same unusual name and address during the month. Even though I was personally handling thousands of requests for forms, I found it necessary to devise a time-consuming checklist for duplicate requests. When I printed a required order form, the problem was eliminated. Certain manufacturers also require forms or mail-in certificates so that they can maintain some sort of control. A certain amount of money is alloted to the refunding promotion, but frequently a major portion of this allotment remains unclaimed. *Please do not abuse the refunding privilege*. As long as sales continue to rise, refunders will prosper. In fact, since my initial television appearance, I have witnessed a dramatic rise in the amount of refunds available both in dollars and in numbers of offers around. I have found it necessary to reduce the print size in *Dollars Daily* to accommodate the increasing number of refund offers.

Beat the system legally. Buy the product, and try it. Please do not rip off the label at the supermarket for a refund. This discourages supermarket managers from displaying refund forms, salesmen from setting up promotional displays, and companies from offering future giveaways. Besides, it definitely is stealing. If you wouldn't take the product, then don't destroy it by removing the universal product code or proof of purchase seal. It isn't fair to the next purchaser, who may also be a refunder or to others not interested in the refunding game but who don't like to purchase ripped-open packages. Don't risk the embarrassment or danger of being prosecuted.

Some refunders exchange extra labels or complete deals with each other. A complete deal is the qualifier and refund form, ready to be mailed. Refunding buddies often hold informal exchange sessions so that they don't remain isolated and can eagerly share refunding information. They become enthusiastic about their new hobby and want everyone to participate in the free promotions. Others enjoy exchanging with advertisers in the classified section of *Dollars Daily*. A bond of fellowship is often formed by mail although exchangers live in distant states and probably will never have the opportunity of meeting each other. Exchanges and round robins help combat the one-to-a-customer rule.

Refunding robins are not chain letters. Chain letters are illegal. They obligate others and may intimidate them into continuing the chain with vague threats. Chain letters or pyramid letters should never be used in the name of refunding. Only those who start the chain stand any chance of cleaning up, while many others waste postage, additional money sent to names on the list, and forms or qualifiers that could have been used for their personal refunding in the vain hope of obtaining something for nothing.

According to the Inspector of the United States Postal Service: "The Postal Service is charged with conducting investigations relating to possible violation of the Mail Fraud Statute, Title 18, United States Code, Section 1341. The Mail Fraud Statute provides substantial fines or imprisonment upon conviction." If you receive a chain letter, either discard it or bring it to your local post office, who will forward it to Washington, D.C. for investigation. Trading forms with fellow refunders is a more constructive method of spending time and postage. Instead of writing twenty copies of a letter in the vain hope of collecting a windfall, send twenty refunds and actually reap profit.

8

Mary Anne's Hotline

Help! I Didn't Receive My Refund!

Don't let a little thing like a rejection slip stop you from refunding. Great writers, actors, artists, and lovers have all experienced rejection before final success. Every refunder has shared the disappointment and frustration of opening an envelope anticipating a refund only to unfold a refusal notice.

A rejection is a form letter from the company or clearinghouse advising that you will *not* be receiving your refund. Usually the appropriate reason is checked.

A typical *Refusal Notice* would read as follows:

Dear Customer:

We regret that it is not possible for us to send your refund at the present time.

Through some misunderstanding or oversight you did not fulfill our requirements as stated in our advertising to which you responded.

In order to be fair to all the thousands of people who have replied to our offer, we must limit the refund to those in full compliance with the respective offer.

Your request is being returned for the following reason. Please resubmit in the proper manner.

_____Original name-and-address form was not enclosed.

_____Cash register tape not enclosed.

_____No proofs of purchase enclosed.

_____Incorrect labels enclosed.

_____Incorrect number of labels enclosed.

_____Improper proof of purchase.

_____Other.

Please do not resubmit your request if it has been returned for any of the following reasons:

_____Duplicate request. Offer limited to one per family or address.

_____Offer expired.

_____Other.

Refund Service
Department

Analyze your rejection letter to see why you will not be rewarded as promised. For example, you may have sent the incorrect qualifier. So many products look alike on supermarket shelves with similar packaging and color or have sound-alike names that it is easy to unknowingly send a competitor's brand. Okay, you are

----

positive you purchased the right brand, and you have
the rest of the package to prove it. Yet the company
claims you sent an incorrect qualifier. Did you send the
portion of the package required? A proof of purchase
seal may or may not be the same as the Universal
Product Code number. If the UPC states proof of
purchase seal, it is correct; if not, scan the package to
see if there is such a marking elsewhere. You bought
the right product and sent the correct portion. What
next? Reread the refund form that has been returned to
you with your rejection. Once I was positive the
company had indeed made an error by refusing my
legitimate request for a refund. For a wild moment I
debated the possibilities of writing to the president of
the company to report this gross injustice or of merely
avoiding that product on all future shopping lists. I
skimmed the form again and for the first time observed
in large block print that a wrapper from my favorite loaf
of bread must be included. Silly? Well, I didn't play the
game by the rules. If you don't touch third base, you
don't score a home run. I just did not qualify for the
refund even though I had purchased the company's
product and sent the correct portion of the label.
Advertising promotions are designed for various reasons, and if they desired a bread wrapper, it was my
duty to send one in order to receive cash back. My
labels were returned with the rejection, so I merely
resubmitted the request as specified this time. Sometimes the offer has expired by the time you receive your
refusal notice. The company will almost always grant
an extension date and perhaps a new box number for
submitting your request. The letter may instruct you to
email the refusal notice with correct qualifiers to the
specified address.

Once in a while, to refunders' dismay, the labels will not be returned because they were inadvertently destroyed before the omission was discovered. But you can't win them all. This is a rare occurrence but nothing to become upset about. Learn from experience, and try to be accurate to prevent labels from going astray in the future.

Another typical reason for a rejection may be that you did not send the required mail-in certificate. Certain companies, like Lender's® bagels, require refund forms as a control of the amount of refunds distributed. They could not afford to stay in business if they refunded every package of bagels sold. However, manufacturers such as Lender's® are very generous. If you still have the label or continue to use the product, jot down the name of the refund offer with its expiration date. Be sure to include the name of the item and the amount of the refund, as well as the date the offer expires for the purpose of exchange.

When exchanging refund offers with the vast network of refunders out there, submit your request list. Most exchangers gladly help beginners; they can recall a distant past when the wonderful world of refunding was opened to them. Don't try to skip the exchange part of refunding. This is where you not only locate that elusive refund form but also find refunding pen pals. Some refunders hold their own swap-session meetings in each other's homes once a week to exchange refunding information, forms, or qualifiers and to display special premiums received so that friends can decide whether to participate in the promotion or not. This not only is a great motivational session but also brings neighbors and family together for a common cause. One subscriber wrote, "My sister is halfway across the country, and we never had anything to write to each other about. But since I've started refunding, we have become very close. A week doesn't pass that we don't exchange letters, and they're always about the same subject."

I remember that when I was growing up I always wanted a pen pal. I finally found one when my best friend moved away. But after a while our letters dropped off because we had nothing in common. When I started refunding, I had many pen pals and I loved receiving their letters because they always contained a surprise, like a Lender's® refund form. It pays to have friends.

I always manage to accumulate a supply of refund forms that I personally cannot utilize, so whenever my pen pals send request lists, I am glad to send the desired form if I have it. You have to be superorganized to locate forms instantly. I arrange them chronologically in a shoebox with little dividers for each month and with the current month in front. You are less apt to miss closing dates and you can tell at a glance whether you have the form or not if you file the forms alphabetically by month. It may take a little time to set up the system but it's easy to maintain and expedient: you are warned about expiration dates that rapidly approach. And a glance should tell you whether the offer is regional or not.

Don't wait until the end of the month or, even worse, the end of the year to do last minute refunding. December 31 is an arbitrary closing date for many refunds and, in the midst of the holiday season, most households are extra busy. If you have the label, use the product, or would like to try it for the first time, now is the time to send in the refund. Don't procrastinate. You may forget about the offer or misplace the form and before you know it, you miss the expiration date. Sending for refunds after the expiration date is a very common reason for rejection.

Read the form carefully, include all requirements, be sure to address it correctly, clearly put your name, address, and ZIP code on the request, pay attention to expiration dates, and you will limit refusal notices. If you don't have the form, try submitting without one. If you receive a rejection for this reason, make a notation of the company's name, and try to remember that forms are required. Just because one company refuses your request without a form, don't assume that all others will do the same. Many pay without forms or will list a special address where you may write to obtain the refund form.

If you will recall the last pad of refund forms you saw on the supermarket shelves, you may have seen a cardboard backing behind the forms. It usually says, "Sorry, all forms are gone" but sometimes it lists an address where you can write to receive the required form or it clearly states that the form is unnecessary as long as you mail the required qualifiers to a certain address. If I have this information, I include it in *Dollars Daily* so that you may immediately mail away for the refund or mandatory form.

Occasionally a refund may be lost in the mail. I've read about people mysteriously receiving letters mailed years ago and delivered without explanation. Once the Englishtown Post Office asked Nana to sign for a fifty-cent refund. This is an extremely unusual occurrence, but someone was apprehended with sacks of mail containing refunds. It is a federal offense to tamper with United States mail but the thought of

SORRY

All the official order forms have been taken. You may obtain one by writing to:

**Free Efferdent Offer
P.O. Box 9512-S
St. Paul, Minn. 55195**

The official order form must accompany your correct proofs of purchase and may not be reproduced. Sorry, no clubs or organizations are eligible. Limit one offer per name or address. Offer good only in U.S.A. and is void where prohibited or otherwise restricted. Requests for the official order form must be received by February 28, 1979. Allow 4-6 weeks for delivery.

This cardboard backing tells you that a form must accompany your qualifiers and gives the address where you may write to get the correct form.

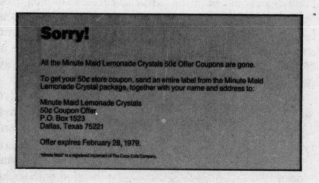

Sorry!

All the Minute Maid Lemonade Crystals 50¢ Offer Coupons are gone.

To get your 50¢ store coupon, send an entire label from the Minute Maid Lemonade Crystal package, together with your name and address to:

Minute Maid Lemonade Crystals
50¢ Coupon Offer
P.O. Box 1523
Dallas, Texas 75221

Offer expires February 28, 1979.

"Minute Maid" is a registered trademark of The Coca-Cola Company.

This cardboard backing tells you where to send your qualifiers so you may get your store coupon without it.

quick silver trapped the thief. The Post Office just wanted to be assured that the correct person finally received each letter in those sacks, and that's why Nana's signature was necessary for a petty refund. Although this was an extraordinary situation, pilfery may be one reason for nonreceipt. On another occasion, I received a refund from Prestone® that was supposed to contain a two dollar bill. Although the envelope was sealed and the mail-in folder cemented tightly, it was empty. I assumed the company must have forgotten to include the bill. However, after checking with Nana and other refunding buddies, I found their envelopes were also empty. This remains an unsolved mystery. It may have been an error.

Refunders who keep careful records write letters to the company (not the clearinghouse) informing them that the refund has not been received. Some refund order blanks have a tear-off receipt, which acts as a record of mailing to help in the event of a missing refund. Companies care and want to know whenever you do not receive a refund as promised so that they may investigate the cause of non-receipt. Most will make good on the offer and even send you extra coupons or gifts to compensate for your disappointment and postage.

If you should receive an expired coupon, write to the manufacturer to advise them of the mishap. Again, all problems should be addressed to the Customer Services Division at the address printed on the package, since the original refunding box number has probably been closed. I received two outdated coupons and was going to chuck them out but reconsidered and mailed them to another favorite of the refunding clan, Green Giant.® I received the following note:

Our Apologies:
Through the human element of error, the wrong coupons were sent.

To compensate for your inconvenience and extra postage, enclosed are three certificates good on your next purchases of Green Giant® Brand Entrees.

It pays to advise the manufacturer when you experience a refunding problem. Now Green Giant® has taken steps to avoid future errors and printed the new coupon without an expiration date.

If you don't receive a refund and have waited a reasonable period of time or have an unhappy experience with your refund, don't hesitate to inform the company.

A Word About One of Our Sponsors

Procter and Gamble may be the refunders' choice as an all-time favorite manufacturer. They will send you almost any form good in your state and also refund your postage if you write to a central post office box. Subscribers report requesting several forms on a single postcard and receiving the forms and full first-class postage back. The only specification Procter and Gamble makes is that you tell them exactly what you would like to receive and request only one of each form. Never say, "Please send all refund offers," for if you do, you will simply receive a form letter minus the forms. Instead, list each specific offer exactly as advertised by the company, including expiration date. Since they have so many regional offers and an extensive list of promotions, you must be precise. For example, a sample request list (now expired) might be, "Please send forms for Downy® children's dinnerware expiring August 31, Tide® $2.00 expiring October 31, and Duncan Hines® Cake Mix expiring September 30." You will probably receive all three forms and extension slips if they arrive close to expiration dates. If your mother would like to receive the same forms, a separate request must be made and mailed separately. Remember, they always return your postage and grant extension slips, so you have nothing to lose.

I find that Procter and Gamble usually pays without forms but many persons feel more confident with the form. This very generous manufacturer also offers another special consideration that I have not yet discovered from any other company. Suppose the refund order blank calls for the net weight statements from two giant-size boxes of Tide®. You may use any combination of boxes as long as you equal or exceed the net weight required. For example, I might submit one king-size net weight and one regular-size net weight as long as I add the total number of ounces. Most manufacturers insist on the specific size requirements of the offer and sometimes will not accept larger, more expensive sizes. However, Procter and Gamble permits you to mix and match sizes as long as the total number of ounces equals or exceeds the refund promotion.

Procter and Gamble also prints a receipt on each mail-in certificate for you to keep for your records. In the event that you do not receive your refund, you merely have to check the receipt for mailing date and address to notify. A typical receipt on a Procter and Gamble refund offer may say, "Help us help you.

Checking, careful handling, and on-time shipment of consumer requests have always been our policy, but sometimes things go wrong. If something should go wrong with your request, remember we want to please you and will make every effort to do so. Just let us know—information from you can help us improve our service. Write any questions or comments concerning this offer to Consumer Services. Please give us your phone number in case we have to call you."

Only once did I have occasion to complain about nonreceipt of a Procter and Gamble promotion. Sure enough, they telephoned an apology and forwarded the refund by return mail. If you happen to receive regional promotions outside your area, Procter and Gamble will make good on their offer. So when vacationing or traveling through other states, be on the lookout for special, local Procter and Gamble promotions.

Dear Coupon Queen:
Many refunds are put out by Procter & Gamble so I wrote them this letter:

Dear Mr. Procter:
I'm taking a GAMBLE and being a little BOLD to see if I would GAIN anything in asking you for refund forms put out by your company. It would SURE THRILL me and save me time and ERA. I always enJOY each of your products for I know it DUZ a TOP JOB. Store owners today keep a SECRET about refunds and are on the SAFEGUARD of people tearing off the labels. They should BOUNCE them out of the store. So if possible

please *DASH* me over some refund forms in the self-addressed, stamped envelope enclosed.

CHEER

Dear *CHEER*:

I love your CHARMIN letter and know it wasn't written in a JIF. Procter and Gamble is a generous company and always sends a bonus of your postage back so the SASE (self-addressed, stamped envelope) is unnecessary. In fact, if you request forms on a postcard, you'll get a speedy reply and full first-class postage back. With the wide SCOPE of mail they receive and the BOUNTY of mail-in certificates they provide, they must always know exactly which refund forms you desire. So in all your ZEST don't forget to list product, amount of refund, and expiration date.

Happy Refunding,
Mary Anne

To quickly sum up what Procter and Gamble does:

1. They often pay without forms.
2. They send forms when required certificates are needed.
3. They permit you to combine net-weight statements from their products.
4. They refund your postage if you must request a form.
5. They will send several offers on each request.

6. They send extension slips if the offer will expire soon.

7. Best of all, they offer fantastic giveaways free.

Another Procter and Gamble bonanza! The Sun-Sational "free gift away" gave you a choice of old and new favorite soaps, and two free gift choices. I decided on the Dazey® Donut Factory and Presto Burger® and was able to clear out my three-year collection of Ivory® soap wrappers.

Procter and Gamble is definitely a major candidate as the refunder's choice for favorite manufacturer. In the illustrated offer, two bars of soap and cash register receipt from your Thanksgiving turkey brought back $1, plus a 50¢ bonus certificate, for a total of a $1.50 cash return. They also gave a 10¢ cash-off incentive to buy the soap and an extension certificate to give you more time. Would you believe the soap happens to be a terrific product? I received a profit to discover a great refreshing soap.

Whenever I need a product that does not offer a current refund, I always favor Procter and Gamble. By now you are wondering if it's all soap and detergents. Well, Nana recalls Oxydol® was a laundry-day reliable when she used a scrub board before the advent of wringer-type washing machines. I still use Procter and

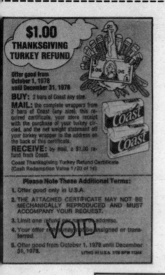

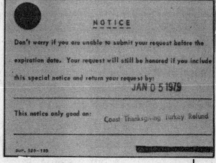

Gamble products in my modern, fully automatic washer. But they are also famous for Pampers® and peanut butter. In case you are wondering whether you ever use Procter and Gamble products, here's a list of some I've enjoyed:

Biz®	Ivory®
Bold®	Jif®
Bonus®	Joy®
Bounce®	Lava®
Bounty®	Lilt®
Camay®	Luvs®
Cascade®	Mr. Clean®
Charmin®	Oxydol®
Cheer®	Pampers®
Coast®	Prell®
Comet®	Pringles®
Crest®	Puffs®
Crisco®	Safeguard®
Dash®	Salvo®
Downy®	Scope®
Dreft®	Secret®
Duncan Hines®	Spic and Span®
Duz®	Sure®
Era®	Thrill®
Fluffo®	Tide®
Folger's®	Top Job®
Gain®	White Cloud®
Gleem®	Wondra®
Head and Shoulders®	Zest®

Procter and Gamble may be the refunder's choice as most generous, but a single issue of *Dollars Daily* will inform you of hundreds of other companies who willingly participate in the refunding game. In fact, it would be safe to say that your own refrigerator, cabinets, and medicine chest probably hold a dozen dollars worth of labels that will probably end in the trash unless you take further action now to rescue found money from the incinerator!

9

Shopping on a Postage Stamp

All-Occasion Gifts and Rebates

Next holiday season let a few postage stamps do the shopping for you. Many refunders report receiving gifts for their entire Christmas shopping list absolutely free. Your closet can harbor a wealth of extras ready for giving whenever the occasion arises. Did an unexpected shower catch you short of spending power this week? Just browse through your storehouse of varied presents, and select an appropriate bridal or baby gift.

Refunds run the gamut from T-shirts to tote bags imprinted with popular, snappy slogans. My son, Jimmy, loves his "Squeeze Me" shirt. My husband, Jim, can't seem to outwear his Tuff Stuff® and Puma® shirts. Tote bags are perfect for both sexes and any age. Cigarette lighters, electric razors, panty hose, cologne, coloring books, hats, and toys are exactly the right gifts for someone. Maybe you quit smoking but still have empty cigarette wrappers hoarded in your precious label file. Think twice before allowing that Cricket® lighter to escape your gift plan for the future. Will it

make a perfect stocking stuffer for someone who hasn'
kicked the habit? If you already have the labels or use
the product anyway, send for free, all-occasion gifts
You will always find a recipient to appreciate your
thoughtfulness.

Don't believe token gifts are the only premiums
available. I received my son's playpen, baby carriage
large, red coaster wagon, Dazey® donut maker, Presto
Burger®, electric mixers, tablecloths, dishes, glass
ware, and tableware settings for twelve through re
funding.

I never buy get-well cards but prefer using post
age to share extra refunds with shut-ins. Would you
rather receive a greeting card or a crisp, two dollar bill?
Sometimes I telephone the person, advising them of the
approaching refund so that they may anticipate its
arrival and know someone is thinking of them in their
period of illness. Other times I grant the mailman the
honor of surprising the recipient. After awhile, you
gain a reputation for sending unsolicited refunds, and
the surprise element is gone forever. However, the
arrival gives the shut-in an excuse to telephone and
share a laugh. Nana has become a clock watcher and
knows precisely when the mailman will stop at her door
now that refunds brighten her otherwise dim cluster of
bills and junk mail.

The pursuit of refunding is wild in the appliance
field. A friend of mine purchased three smoke-detector
units on sale for twelve dollars each. She received a
rebate check for fifteen dollars: five dollars for each unit
purchased. She spent a total of thirty-six dollars and
received fifteen dollars in cash back by mailing a single
request requiring only one postage stamp. Rebates are
the best refunds you can obtain.

ebates are refund offers. In fact, they offer the greatest
mount of money back. Of course, purchases with rebates are
ot everyday purchases, but they should not be overlooked
when we need the item ourselves or are considering buying a
ift for others.

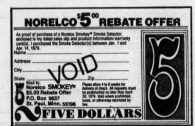

Alert refunders cash in on the avalanche of rebate offers at appliance centers. Anyone who has attended a bridal shower during the past few years knows appliances reign supreme. When Mom was married she had an old-fashioned linen shower and received a surplus of tea towels. Today, large, expensive gifts are in vogue but linens are often avoided because of their prohibitive price range and problem of choice. You must cope with perplexing problems of pattern and color that will compliment and not clash with room decor. Then you are required to snoop and find out whether the new bride prefers a twin, full, queen, or a king-size bed. Appliances are desirable and exchangeable, should an identical gift arrive. Refunds float about for all national-brand appliances, ranging from toasters to refrigerators. You always receive your cash back no matter where the item is purchased, so be sure to check for sales and low prices at discount stores. Linens will continue to fade in the foggy past as gifts for bridal showers until manufacturers decide to jump on the refunding bandwagon.

I save shipping costs on my brother's birthday gifts by having the company forward a premium gift directly to his Vermont address. His present is not gift-wrapped, but he enjoys a gift in a higher price range than I could afford if I had to pay for the gift plus shipping charges.

Refunders often wonder about what course to follow when a premium gift arrives broken. The practical thing to do is to advise the company of the damaged merchandise. Again, you do not write to the box number on the refund form since the offer may have expired or the clearinghouse may be backlogged, but write to the consumer services division of the company itself (address taken from product label). Wait and see! The following apology and replacement dishes were forwarded almost immediately.

The Procter and Gamble Company
Cincinnati, Ohio
March 8, 1979

It must have been very disappointing to receive your order and find it had been damaged. We're sorry.

Our Promotion people take great care in packing our premiums to help insure their safe arrival, and I regret your shipment did not receive this same care en route to you. This happens occasionally despite the efforts we take in protecting each item.

I'm processing a new order for you, and it should arrive in about three weeks. We hope you'll be completely satisfied with the replacement children's dinnerware bowls. Meanwhile, I'm enclosing a postage refund for your letter to us.

Sincerely,

Consumer Services

Refunders often ask me what are the biggest refunds I have ever heard about. There are many, ranging from automobile rebates to actual refunds on cruise fares to cash-back offers for elegant, enduring diamonds.

Kellogg's® offered a free child's Amtrak ticket anywhere in the United States for three cereal box tops and the purchase of an adult full-fare ticket. There are refund promotions on major appliances such as washing machines, dryers, dishwashers, stoves, and microwave ovens. If you are in the market for all new kitchen appliances, you may actually receive one appliance free of charge. However, if you need only one, you may obtain fifty dollars back from the company. Rebates on television sets, Citizen Band radios, tape decks, and stereos with auxiliary speakers are commonplace today.

Advertising agencies invent ingenious giveaways guaranteed to tempt your pocketbook. This year, an Instamatic® camera brought Santa Claus down from the North Pole to personally visit your youngster at home on Christmas Eve. Or if you preferred, you could have received his suit free of charge, so Santa could visit your child every year. As money decreases in value in today's inflated world, concrete items take on value.

My brother, Pat, recently relocated to Vermont. I'm glad he has a great future with his new job at I.B.M., but those long-distance calls were killing my budget. Post® cereal offered a free telephone call to any number in the United States for box tops, so refunding paid for a very lengthy long-distance phone call from Lakehurst, New Jersey to Vermont. Now if he eats his breakfast, and saves the box tops, Pat can call me back. And if Mom will switch from eggs to cereal, she can call him. I wonder how long we can keep this telephone chain going?

There is fantastic competition in the refunding race for your dollar, and manufacturers continue to create superlative challenges. Large purchases mean large refunds. False economy can actually limit your refunds. Instead of purchasing an inferior coffee maker, buy the best brand around and receive a cash rebate for doing so. Refunding power will help you to afford new appliances before the old ones have finally conked out, a surprise visit from Santa, or even overdue, long-distance telephone calls to loved ones.

Dabbling in refunding will bring quarters back, but diving into it wholeheartedly brings in dollars daily. Consider all possibilities on appliance rebates before making that final decision on your next gift purchase.

Don't skim over personal care products, because hair dryers, blowers, curling irons, dental hygiene units, cosmetic cases, and electric razors all join the ranks of items that offer rebates.

The key to holiday gift giving with refunds is to start early enough. Right now is the perfect time to begin collecting free gifts for a coming birthday or holiday. One refunder wrote, "This is the first year I actually have money left over after Christmas shopping." Another correspondent sent the following letter, listing the items she obtained after a few months of the refunding hobby.

> *Dear Coupon Queen:*
> *I have found a way to save money on Christmas shopping. We give to over thirty relatives, and it is very costly.*

My two daughters and I went through Dollars Daily and picked out many of the free gifts. We then decided to whom we would like to give them. My daughters were very eager to help with the grocery shopping because they knew that with the labels from the groceries their favorite people would be getting a present. I find them very willing to try new products. This is a sample of how we are doing our Christmas giving:

Daddy–Chap Stick® travel-size shaving cream and deodorant
Charlie–Kellogg's® road atlas
Gram–Dermassage® apron
Aunt Frieda–Chex® decanter and tumbler
Nana–Purina® calendar
Cousin Laura–Special Dinners® necklace
Cousin Jenny–Fruit Loops® puzzle
Uncle Ken–Raid® barbecue cookbook
Aunt and Unkee–Sunsational® Gift-a-Way popcorn popper
Cat–Tender Vittles® heart-shaped cat dish
Dog–Purina® puppy kit.

Santa's Helper

Dear Santa's Helper:

Great! You even saved time shopping in the stores to buy these gifts. Sorry we had to cut your list down, but if any of your relatives are reading this book, we'll ruin your surprises.

Refunding as a Fund Raiser

Refunding is a successful alternative to traditional bake sales, newspaper drives, and white-elephant sales as a money maker for fund-raising committees.

Even large charities, like the famous Jerry Lewis Muscular Dystrophy campaign, raise money through refunding. They participate a little differently than we do. Sara Lee® or Schick® (the sponsor) will offer a refund promotion and donate the refund to this charity. It is a completely painless way for consumers to donate and show that half dollars actually do add up. For example, this holiday season, Schick® printed a refund requesting a particular qualifier. For each one received, they donated fifty cents to Jerry Lewis' pet project. Sara Lee® had a promotion that offered you fifty cents back and an additional fifty cents for Jerry's Kids. Other companies frequently give you the choice of receiving cash back or donating it to charity.

Refunding is the most neglected method of fund raising. Schools are now discovering Campbell's® Labels for Education programs and the Colgate® School Action Plan whereby labels are collected on a school-wide basis for equipment not approved for purchase by frugal boards of education. Post® cereals offered a vast assortment of play equipment, and with all those youngsters munching cereal every morning, schools really were able to extend their physical-education supplies. When spring fever hits school children, there never seem to be enough volley balls or jump ropes to go around. However, large school equipment like monkey bars, basketball courts, Ping-Pong® tables and badmitton equipment are all possible with a united school effort.

Churches, missions, Scout troups, P.T.A. organizations and other nonprofit groups are latching onto refunding as their ways and means. Other than the specialized group promotions such as the Post® cereal, Colgate®, or Campbells® programs, refunding may still be limited to one refund per family or address. Therefore, refunds must be mailed by members of the committee in their own names and addresses and then the proceeds are donated toward the community project. A committee chairperson is essential to coordinate the program. With a little know-how, organization, and lots of cooperation, the project can be a real fund raiser. Some groups mimeograph a current list of qualifiers listed in *Dollars Daily* and pass these out to the membership. Others merely post a list of desired qualifiers on the bulletin board.

Label collection is an easy method to supplement proceeds from the annual church supper and increase that diminishing club treasury.

10

Couponmania

The Most Often Asked Questions and the Coupon Queen's Favorite Fan Mail

Dear Coupon Queen:
When you bought $120 worth of groceries for only $.79, didn't you have to pay the $120 and then send in something to different companies for money back on the product?
                                                    Skeptical

Dear Skeptical:
No! I never pay more than $10 a week for groceries to feed my family. We save all our labels, so when a refund comes out for freebies, I mail the qualifiers. Once you start refunding you will discover it is one big cycle and there always will be a new refund out for the same items.
I just cashed my free coupons for the $120 in groceries. The $.79 was for tax, which is never refundable. The cashier rings up the total and then deducts the coupons. I would

never have that much money with me to pay
such a large bill at the supermarket.

Dear Coupon Queen:

They say seeing is believing. I saw you
buy $71.71 worth of grociers for $7.19 but can't
believe you did a week's shopping for this little
bit of money. You must have had a lot of junk
foods and things you wouldn't buy if you
didn't have a coupon.

Nonbeliever

Dear Nonbeliever:

Mike Douglas is a believer. He wanted to
know what kinds of food fill my shopping cart.
He saw milk, eggs, fresh fruit, steaks, seafood, canned and frozen vegetables, prepared
spaghetti sauce, and very few snacks. I send
for any type of cat food refunds because Sandy
is a true refunder and willingly switches
brands. However, I can't take advantage of all
dog food offers because Skippy is choosy.

I like to serve my family the basic food
groups and steer clear of junk foods except for
parties and other special times.

Dear Coupon Queen:

What type of magazine or newspaper
should I buy to find refund offers? The only
kind I ever see is for ten cents off an expensive
product.

Bewildered

Dear Bewildered:

You don't buy any extra magazines or newspapers other than those you are now reading. The very newspaper you buy probably features refund forms ready for the easy-money game. Wednesday or Thursday papers with weekly supermarket specials are the issues to watch. Sunday supplements frequently have several refund offers. I have found refund forms in every magazine conceivable, ranging from Psychology Today *to* Field and Stream, Co-Ed, Popular Mechanics *and even* Prevention *magazine. Of course, the popular women's service magazines like* Family Circle, *available right in the supermarket, will offer the most refunds.*

The ten-cent coupons you refer to are cash-offs that you bring directly to the grocery for redemption. Refund offers are always for much greater value, usually ranging from a minimum of fifty cents to five dollars for various purchases. You must mail away to receive these refunds or rebates. Once you become aware of refund forms, you will notice them everywhere. Don't forget the form is not always required, so all you need is the information as published in magazines and newspapers and special refunding publications like Dollars Daily *and blank paper.*

Dear Coupon Queen:

I saved the proof of purchase seal on Listerine® *and now find two offers for the*

----

same product calling for different parts of the label, which I threw away.

Why do they print a proof of purchase seal if they don't intend to use it?

Space Saver

Dear Space Saver,

Manufacturers are notorious for changing refund requirements. Pampers® just changed their qualifiers, and I was caught short this time since I also thought I could save space by saving the small size oval that had previously been necessary for redemption. We all fall into this cleanup trap. Don't be upset, but try to learn from the experience. I'm sure the company's intentions are for us to buy the product because of the refund offer. They are aware of our squirreling antics, so they also play the game by switching qualifiers as we switch brands. I have collected from the front label glued on a bottle of Listerine,® back label, proof of purchase seal, UPC symbol, pull tab, and, after receiving all these cash rebates, ended up with a coupon for a free bottle. I now have a complete wrapper and label ready to go once a new offer is announced.

I know you may think it's a waste of space when we save entire wrappers on speculation, but it's the only way to collect on all refunds the company issues.

Dear Coupon Queen:

I have just started receiving Dollars Daily *and have some questions: (1) Why can't I find offers or forms in the supermarkets where I shop? and (2) Do you send for big-money coupons or just coupons for food?*

Quiz Kid

Dear Quiz Kid:

(1) Some store managers just aren't aware of the fact that their customers are interested in refund forms and don't realize the potential for higher results on shelf items. I frequently see salesmen setting up special displays with a large quantity of products that will provide qualifiers for refunds. Perhaps certain areas or stores are favored for such displays because of volume of sales. Many customers have spoken to store managers with success. Store managers are now becoming aware of refund forms and contact the salesman who can supply pads of forms.

(2) Yes! I certainly do send for big-money coupons, that's how I earned my title. I send for every refund offer I can use. I will switch brands for big-money coupons that really slash your grocery bill. Some just specify turkey, ground beef, produce, fruit, or any brand of snacks such as chips. If you have the labels or use the product, definitely send for the refund.

Dear Coupon Queen:
     Please tell your readers that when they stock up on merchandise to store it in a safe, dry place. When paper towels offered premiums, I bought enough to get several Instamatic® cameras absolutely free. Unfortunately, for the first time in the history of our house, the basement flooded after a severe storm. On the first sunny day my clothesline, with reams of paper towels drying on it, was a funny sight for neighbors. I rescued every paper towel and have a picture to prove it.
                                        All Wet

Dear All Wet:
     Thanks for the tip. Sometimes you can buy the quantity of items all at once if they are not perishable to get an immediate refund or premium for less than the cost of the item. Recently many subscribers bought soap on sale with cash-offs, paying very little and receiving fantastic gifts from Procter and Gamble.® The current retail price of the promotion item was more than their actual soap cost. I suppose Procter and Gamble® buys its promotion giveaway items in such large quantity that their actual unit cost is much less than what we would pay for a single appliance at a discount center.

Dear Coupon Queen:
     I have been having a lot of success receiving refunds without using forms. Now I have one question. Does the cardboard back-

ing of the refund forms for the Kool-Aid®
cannister offer say "no form needed"? I received a refusal notice, but since then I've
noticed your note in the Coupon Queen Special. Should I try again?

Puzzled

Dear Puzzled:

Thank you for bringing this to my attention. I wrote a letter to Kool-Aid®, and this
part of their response:

"It appears that a clerical error was
made in returning your request. With the
hundreds of thousands of requests processed
by this office each week, we find on occasion
that errors do occur. Unfortunately, you were
on the receiving end of our unintentional
error, and we do apologize.

Therefore, if you will please return your
entire request to this address, we will try to
make an adjustment to your satisfaction.

Again, our apologies for the error and
any inconvenience caused you and thank you
for your interest in our products and promotions."

General Foods Corp.

Dear Coupon Queen:

You gave me a great idea when I saw you
on the news and, if I can inspire someone else,
I feel I owe it to you. I can't thank you enough
for going public and sharing your refunding
gold mine with your fellow citizens. You'll

never know how appreciative we are, for a very special reason: three actually.

Two years ago in July, we received three foster sons, all brothers. At the time, we didn't dare hope for a permanent relationship, but Michael, Timothy, and Robert officially became free for adoption. Then another problem arose. In our financial bracket it was impossible for us to swing it, no matter how we figured it. Our caseworkers were wonderful, so human and so helpful. A new law was passed concerning adoption of sibling groups. We had a talk with our lawyer, and he, knowing our financial situation, told us he'd handle the adoptions of all three boys, and we could pay at our convenience.

Believe it or not I started refunding at the end of February and shortly received over $160 to go into a special fund to adopt our boys. Our lawyer is being paid on the installment plan with refunds. When I saw you on the 11 PM news, you gave me the idea for extra income and a way we might raise the money to pay for legal fees to make our family whole and permanent. Boy, does it ever work!

Our fellas, four, eight, and eleven, are really involved in refunding also. Our four-year-old loves to go down our drive to get the mail to see if Mommy has any coupons or refunds. They never throw anything away until they've asked me if I can use the label. Our eleven-year-old brought home an empty Hawaiian Punch® can on the last day of school because he just knew Mommy could use the label. He was right! The boys know we're paying for their adoptions with refunds, and they tell everyone about it. Some people look like they think we are flipped, but little do they know that they are missing out on all the fun and profit.

Mary Anne, the boys thank you, I thank you, and my husband, Andy, thanks you. The Coupon Queen has definitely had a hand in making our foster family a permanent family, and we couldn't be happier.

God bless you.

> Sincerely,
> Evelyn

Dear Evelyn:

I really enjoyed reading your letter, and I'm glad refunding is helping your family grow together.

Dear Coupon Queen:

I went to my sister's apartment for the first time this weekend. She started to throw things away that I could use, so I immediately opened the trash and started washing sour cream containers, collecting snack wrappers, etc. I made a doggie bag of labels to bring home with me.

She told me I could have anything in the apartment I could use—except my new brother-in-law!

> Sister Sue

Dear Sister Sue:

There certainly is fun in refunding. I guess even refunders must draw the line somewhere!

Dear Coupon Queen:

Ever since I received my first issue of Dollars Daily, my life has changed and so has my figure. At first, I must admit I didn't understand all the lingo and ways of refunding. After a few days of reading Dollars Daily over and over, it all started to come together in my head. Well, I started running out to the stores making extra trips everyday, hunting forms and specially marked packages. I was so busy setting up a filing system, running to the post office, mailing things out, answering ads in Dollars Daily, going through my two months' stack of newspapers in storage in the basement, clipping, clipping, clipping refund coupons, that I lost six pounds.

I've been so busy with my new hobby, thanks to you, that I haven't been munching between meals. I'm overjoyed. I needed to lose a few pounds. So I'm making money, cutting my grocery bill, and losing weight with my new refunding hobby!

Twiggy

Dear Twiggy:

Many people snack when they are bored or have nothing to do. I am glad refunding has helped you lose weight. I don't personally have a weight problem but do empathize with those who have a lifetime struggle juggling grapefruit and protein and yet seem to gain weight.

Dear Coupon Queen:

I'm new at refunding, so I'm a bit lost. The other day I was sorting labels and covered the bed in the spare bedroom with them. As my boys were passing the room, I heard my eight-year-old instruct the preschooler, "Don't go in there and touch anything or you'll ruin Mommy's puzzle."

Lost in a Maze

Dear Lost:

It's wonderful that the boys respect your hobby. I hope this book helps you organize so that more refunds will be at your fingertips. Most refunders dislike filing but love receiving fat envelopes. Your sons are correct. Refunding is a gigantic puzzle and fun to solve, matching qualifier and refund form and fitting pieces together for mailing.

Every business must have a filing system. Perhaps the boys will be able to help you sort qualifiers. Once the little guy learns the alphabet, he can match brand names. Filing labels is a terrific approach to teaching reading skills. Children are always eager to help. Try to include them in your filing chores. The entire family reaps benefits, and they will not only respect your hobby but also gain a better understanding of it.

Dear Coupon Queen:

Since I saw you on television, I have learned to save everything but potato peels, and I hear people are even saving them to plant potatoes in the garden.

Recycler

Dear Recycler:

There is too much waste in the world today. My grandmother saved string and bits of yarn, which became toys for us to play with. The ecology minded will be glad to learn how to recycle labels and wrappers into cash, coupons, and free gifts.

Dear Coupon Queen:

We all enjoy shopping these days. The children look for forms, while my husband and I locate products to go with the free coupons. By the way, forms have become so popular in our neighborhood that our grocers show a sign when forms come in, making shopping even more fun.

I have found that some larger companies will accept photocopies if accompanied by the right proof of purchase indicated on the form.

Form Alert

Dear Alert:

Wow! I hope other grocery managers will follow suit and be as cooperative. Their total sales will increase because of the refund announcement. It's amazing how many forms are right before your eyes once you are aware of them. The never-ending hunt is a challenge. Refunders are enterprising in their ways of locating forms and generously share extras. That's how Dollars Daily *created the Free Form Club for beginning subscribers who can't find forms.*

I've heard from other subscribers that companies often accept copies. However, I don't have access to a copy machine, so I haven't personally tried it.

Those who share their extra forms with fellow refunders find the spirit of giving is fantastic. St. Nick, himself, would be proud of refunders who demonstrate the spirit of Christmas all year long.

Dear Coupon Queen:

On a recent walk around my neighborhood, I spied two Cracker Jack® boxes lying on the lawn. Since they were empty, I quickly removed the outer labels. My friend looked at me strangely, but I explained, "All's fair in love and refunding."

Compulsive

Dear Compulsive:

I know exactly how you feel. It's an irresistible impulse. Next time ask your friend if he saw a dollar bill lying unclaimed on the street, would he leave it there or pick it up.

Refunders are on a perpetual antilitter campaign. Whenever I see a gum wrapper dumped by the curb I think of my electric mixer, which I earned by saving gum wrappers. People who litter with labels and wrappers are not helping to keep America green and certainly not helping to put a little green in their own pockets.

Dear Coupon Queen:

I received my first issue of **Dollars Daily** today and already sent for ten dollars in refunds my first day.

However, I'm wondering if you could give me some advice about how to mark cash register tapes for offers that require them.

Also why would a company issue a refund for a code number?

Coupon Clipper

Dear Coupon Clipper:

I'm glad your subscription paid for itself so quickly.

Some refunders are lucky and have computer readouts on their grocery tapes. The UPC symbol is passed over the computer, and the cash register rings up the sale price, the name, and the size of the item. However, traditional cash registers just ring up prices. I merely circle the correct price with a fine liner, write the name of the product on the receipt, and mail it with the form and other required proofs of purchase.

Many times companies only require code numbers from products. Sometimes the item is an aerosol can or plastic bottle with printing right on the plastic. There is nothing to mail away. Some manufacturers like to receive a copy of the ingredients. I guess they figure that if you take time to copy a list of all the ingredients, you probably will buy the product and try it.

Dear Coupon Queen:

My telephone hasn't stopped ringing since I wrote an article about my refunding experiences of the last four months. I was a fairly normal, sane shopper until February when my husband called me into the living room to see you on the six o'clock news on television. Since I didn't have a pencil to get your address as it flashed on the screen, I returned to my dishes. The eleven o'clock news carried the same interview. Again I watched, yet wrote nothing. The next night was the clincher. The TV station had been inundated with calls for a repeat performance and more information. This time I was ready.

I feel like playing a tape with the repeated message of your name and address to answer all the readers of the Poughkeepsie Journal who keep calling me. I wish the newspaper had printed your address.

Barbara

Dear Barbara: I know how a demanding telephone can temporarily halt refunding and everything else. It's like a baby's cry that must be answered immediately. Thank you for sending a copy of the article with your letter. I

love reading about subscribers' experiences.
The refunding craze is spreading nationally
like wildfire. Everyone likes to get something
for nothing, and that is what refunding is all
about.

Dear Coupon Queen:

You must be doing a good job telling the
housewives in our area about the money they
can save by watching for coupons and refund
offers. It seems that every day someone is
asking for a tear-off form for some refund
offer or another.

My problem, as director of merchandis-
ing for a seven-store, independent supermarket chain, is that I am not always made aware
of all the refund offers that are available from
various manufacturers. Here's where you can
help. Enclosed find a check to cover a one-year
subscription to your publication, Dollars
Daily. Perhaps if I can tell the sales repre-
sentatives what tear-offs should be available,
I will have more success in obtaining them. I
realize that not all offers are good all over as
there are many regional brands, but perhaps I
will be able to better serve our customers with
the information your paper provides.

To make it easier for our customers, we
have installed special bulletin boards near the
front of each of our stores solely for the
purpose of displaying refund offer tear-off
pads. We do this to keep our shelves from
getting cluttered with papers and to discour-

age the taking of entire pads by children and noninterested shoppers.

> Sincerely,
> Director of Merchandising

Dear Director:

I know your customers will benefit through the efforts you are using to help and please them. I hope that store managers in other locations will follow your lead and watch sales zoom on refundable products. Thanks.

Dear Coupon Queen:

As a new refunder, I've been meticulously saving everything. One morning before work I decided to clean up the clutter and started soaking labels off jars. As I removed each label, I washed the glue off the back and laid them right side up on the counter to dry. When I came home from work, I found all my labels very nicely glued to my counter top.

I had to scrub them and peel them off. I learned a valuable lesson well: When leaving labels to dry, put them right side down.

> *Ms. Clean*

Dear Ms. Clean:

Beginning refunders, beware of this common error unless you want your counter decor to match your hobby. Some refunders dry labels on paper toweling or plastic wrap and leave them attached for easy filing.

Dear Coupon Queen:

You are mentioned as the "Queen" of coupons. Maybe someday I will be the "King" of coupons. Sometimes people laugh when I exchange coupons, but I know the register subtracts, so I have the last laugh.

King Charles I

Dear King Charles I:

You are not alone in vying for the championship as Coupon King. Many men are dedicated refunders. I get personal notes from busy physicians, pharmacists, engineers, attorneys, accountants, fire fighters, and even a fellow who has a seat on the stock exchange. Maybe shopping was once left to the little woman, but with today's high finance at the supermart, men are cashing just as many coupons and taking a more active role in shopping.

I can tell you a true story about a dentist who had never gone on a shopping expedition until his wife was in the hospital with a brand-new baby. "I was so embarassed," he said. "I was the only person in the store without a wad of coupons in my hand." Look around—everyone uses coupons today.

In order to shop as I do, the coupons must be for free merchandise obtained from refunds. Seven- or ten-cent cash-offs may actually raise your grocery bill as it did mine. Refunders want to slash that soaring grocery bill and not add to it.

Dear Coupon Queen:

Refunding fever has really hit me, and I hunt for forms in stores as second nature. I usually shop in the same store, but when I get the opportunity, I now run through a "strange" store with a cruising eye. The other day I was able to get different forms in a new store I went into on impulse. I also visit the health-aids section of each department store. When I find an offer in Dollars Daily that appeals to me, I find it easier to write it on a slip of paper as a reminder.

Am I getting there?

Ship Mate

Dear Ship Mate:

Set sails straight ahead! The surest way to navigate the rocky waves of shopping days is to visit different stores and try new products.

Too many get into a shopping rut, stroll down the same aisles picking up the same containers month after month. Add a little spice and variety to your meals and put a little fun into shopping. Assume that adventuresome spirit that makes everyone love refunding. Happy sailing.

Dear Coupon Queen:

I am a new refunder, and to build up a good amount of labels, I conducted a label contest on the school bus I drive. In one month's time my fifty-five students from kindergarten to sixth grade brought in over 4,000 labels. I gave three dollars to the winning student (a fourth-grade girl) who brought in around 1,500 labels herself. It was a good time for all, not to mention the way it built up my supply of qualifiers. I have already received refunds to more than cover the three-dollar prize money.

Bus Number One

Dear Bus Number One:

That's a lightning start on the road to refunding. Many refunders begin by having others save qualifiers for them but soon lose their source as the others see how their trash converts to treasure.

Dear Coupon Queen:

I've become a form addict thanks to your terrific Dollars Daily. After receiving my first issue, I began to search the shelves of my favorite supermarket for forms. After hunting for a couple of weeks and never finding any, I complained to the management.

Lo and behold! The following week I found several pads of forms in almost every aisle. Please tell your readers that it really does pay to speak up. Store managers like to please customers.

Princess Dee

P. S. I've sent away already for more than 130 refunds and new products. I'm beginning to *feel like a coupon queen already. Whenever I complain of a headache now, my husband says it's from that crown pushing its way out of my head.*

Dear Princess Dee:

Today I also received a letter from another subscriber, the jolly Green Giant.® According to Green Giant® you must speak up.

"If there are special forms, which you would desire, please contact the grocery stores where you shop and we are sure they will get in touch with the Green Giant® representative in your area, who in turn will see that forms are put out for these special offers."

Remember, the squeaky wheel gets the grease.

Dear Coupon Queen:

I had an amusing incident during my first week of refunding. I sent in the required number of labels for cat litter. When I received the envelope addressed to me, I was so excited at my first response to a refund letter.

However, I was embarrassed when I read the letter, which very nicely stated they could not refund money for their number-one competitor in the kitty litter field.

Red

Dear Red:

So many product names sound alike and we become so eager that we sometimes don't

*check carefully. There is a new, ready-to-eat
spaghetti product flooding the market. Even I
had trouble in the supermarket selecting the
brand with the free coupon offer since all the
names were so similar.*

Dear Coupon Queen:

It's funny how refund forms suddenly
seem to appear everywhere when you are
looking for them. I never saw one before
reading Dollars Daily. This week I found
forms in a shoe store, yarn shop, crafts store,
automobile department, garden department,
appliance store, as well as the magazines in
my own magazine rack in the living room.

I couldn't personally use all the forms I
saw, but I took several of each form to trade
with form exchangers in the classified section.

Thanks to you, I sent for a total of
seventy-five dollars in refunds. Bermuda here
I come!

Wanderer

Dear Wanderer:

It's a good idea to keep a record of all
refunds so that you can really appreciate how
profitable refunding can be. It's just like
searching for a particular item you want to
buy. Nana wanted a Rival® electric meat
slicer so that her roast beef would be paper
thin like that at the delicatessen. I searched
many stores and finally had to beg the sales-
person to sell me the display model at regular
price, which was dusty and was minus its

guarantee and original carton. After Nana used the meat slicer, I found ads for the same model in all the newspapers and sealed cartons in every chain store I visited. I can't explain the phenomenon, but it does happen every time. Now that you are aware of refund forms, you definitely will find them in the strangest places, even the employee's bulletin board en route to the ladies' room.

Dear Coupon Queen:

Just to show you how much we are wrapped up in refunding, I had been looking all over for a Rath® canned ham for the refund. I searched all the local grocery stores and couldn't find one anywhere. One night, I dreamed that I found the only Rath® ham left in the refrigerated section of my usual supermarket. I can't remember when I've gotten up so cheerfully. I thought I had really found one.

Dreamer

Dear Dreamer:

Whenever my mother misplaces something, she will try to forget about it after unsuccesfully searching all over and go to sleep. Sometimes in the middle of the night her semiconscious mind will tell her exactly where the item can be located. Sometimes I awaken to remember a refund about to expire at the end of the month that I didn't mail yet.

Supermarkets today can't afford to carry all brands. That's why I shop around. Some-

times we still can't find a particular item in our locality. That's the time to switch from ham to turkey, which may have a refund. If you really prefer ham, buy your favorite brand but save the label. You may collect on that one sometime.

Dear Coupon Queen:

I read your article in the September 1, 1978 Family Circle and immediately subscribed to Dollars Daily. After two months of refunding, I went shopping. Although my bill amounted to $57, I only had to pay $28. Do you think if everyone started doing this manufacturers will stop refund offers because of all your recent publicity.

Worried

Dear Worried:

The only letters I received from manufacturers were complimentary, thanking me for promoting their refund offers to the public. Since I was on television, product sales have zoomed and so have the amounts of refund offers. There are so, so many more offers now that I found it necessary to reduce the size print in Dollars Daily to accommodate all of them. In the past, I have printed two hundred offers per month, but now that figure must rise substantially.

Dear Coupon Queen:

Enclosed are a few extra forms for the Free Form Club. Actually, there's a story that *goes with these forms. You never met me, but I've heard so much about you personally that I feel as though we've met. You see, I am a home economics teacher at your hometown high school along with Mrs. B., your former home economics teacher. I was delighted to hear about your experiences in home economics and how you're using the training you received in high school. I was so excited that I brought a copy of* Dollars Daily *to show Mrs. B. I also shared it with the principal, assistant principal, and many fellow teachers. Mrs. B. remembers you well and was pleased to read about your success at refunding.*

As for myself, I have been refunding since last February. I'm so glad you are sharing all your trade secrets. It's become the topic of many conversations at home and at school. My favorite stop on the tour of my new home is my refunding room. It's brimming at the seams with boxes and labels, forms, envelopes, and copies of Dollars Daily. *I have been sharing my new-found skills with other teachers at school, and we now have formed a coupon-and-form exchange.*

The excitement hasn't stopped there, either. I started a label-collection contest with my students, who are responding over-whelmingly. The five-dollar prize for the most labels has been quite an incentive!

As a chapter adviser to the Future Homemakers of America, I have been telling my members about the wonderful world of

----

refunding. They started bringing in labels by the bagful and are anxious to raise money to send the chapter to the state Future Homemakers of America Leadership Convention in March.

Teachers and students have been contributing extra labels and box tops to me. That's where I got these forms for the Free Form Club.

I am so glad you have shared your knowledge with others.

Mrs. R.

Dear Mrs. R.:

Refunding is an alternative to traditional cake sales for fund raising. Post® Cereals, Campbell's® Soup Labels for Education and the Colgate-Palmolive® School Action Plan are designed to help schools. A committee of interested persons can be delegated to collect labels and search and send for offers in order to meet the goal of the organization. Churches, scout groups, and senior citizen clubs are discovering that refunding can finance their projects.

Happy Refunding$

Dear Coupon Queen:

My Gran-Gran loves you. Her name is Betty. I am sending you an article from People *magazine. Thank you for helping us eat cheaper and better.*

Angel

Dear Angel:

You are Grandma's little angel for helping her to refund. Refunding has no age limits. It intrigues toddlers, big girls like you, and senior citizens.

Grandma Betty wrote a letter and said, "I'm the grandmother in a shoe with so many grandchildren, I don't know what to do."

But she does pretty well refunding!

REFUNDER'S PIE

Ingredients
1 refunder   several handfuls forms, qualifiers,
1 pair scissors   *Dollars Daily*, refund newspaper
stamps   (essential to quality of finished
envelopes   product)
         Coffee/tea (optional but supportive)

Assemble above ingredients on a flat surface. Turn on the heat (under coffee or tea) if you selected to use the option. Fill in the necessary requirements, and season with patience for four- to six-week replies. Be sure to check the mail box daily. This pie is filled with honest values and flavored with much satisfaction; if followed carefully the recipe will serve you and your family with extra nutrition (free foods), minerals (silver coins), and exercise (mailbox trips).

For some it could be considered their meat and potatoes (main dish), for occasional participants it is simply a treat, but for many it is a piece of cake.

------------11------------
On the Road to Refunding

Mary Anne's Pep Talk Before the Game

You have decided to use refunding as your weapo
against galloping prices at the supermarket. You wi
never discard another label or empty package withou
considering its monetary value in combating mile-lon
cash register receipts. Remember, both sexes and an
age can play the refunding game, and you always co
lect on GO. What other game can proclaim you a winne
in each event? Set your goals! Do you want a cruise t
the Bahamas or a washer-dryer combination, or do yo
have an insurance premium overdue? When you
cookie jar jingles with silver dollars, halves, an
quarters, it is time to open that vacation savings clu
or start an account for the secret dream you've bee
harboring. Everyone fantasizes about sailing to
tropical paradise or training for a new career if onl
they could afford to do so. Grandpa Andy daydreame
of a distant land of sunshine and palm trees while h
shoveled snow during the winter of his life. They sa

he joys of anticipation are greater than those of
ealization, but I say seeing is believing.

Refunders report that refunding gives them the
ays and means of supporting other hobbies and
nterests, like a trip to see a Broadway play. Whittling
emands wood and carving tools, jogging requires
pecialized sneakers, tennis lessons call for a definite
ash outlay, and my own favorite pastimes, needlework
nd crafts can be ultra-expensive. I store a portion of
y refunds for yarn, crewel kits, and crochet patterns.
oday everything costs money except my money-
aking hobby, which brings dollars daily to my mail-
ox.

You can never solve all your money hassles, but
ou can ease the trauma of budget crunch created by
od shopping by collecting cash from what you for-
erly considered trash. You don't have to buy more
an what your family needs or can use. You let your
rchases count by turning empty wrappers into cool
sh and coupons for free products.

Never skimp on fifty-cent refunds, thinking that
ey are unworthy of your efforts. If you want to pro-
ed full steam ahead on the road to refunding, you
nnot afford to overlook fifty-cent refunds, which can
d up to an annual vacation. Never feel you are
uandering a label on a small refund. A short time
o you would have thrown out the qualifier without a
cond thought, and now you see dollar signs in every
ndy wrapper. Don't hold back qualifiers waiting for
vish refunds. Refunding is not a gamble; you always
n. Suppose you discover a refund for a product
ter you mailed your label for only a small refund. Why
et about fifty cents already in the piggy bank? Just
y another bottle, and take advantage of the new offer

for a free coupon. Now you have participated in both refunds, have the product on the shelf ready for use, have taken a small step toward that vacation fund, and have a new coupon ready for action.

Double coupon days at the supermarket are incentives to empty that wallet full of fifty-cent coupons. In case you've never heard the term before, here's how it works. Some supermarkets occasionally designate a special day during which you receive twice the cash value of each of your coupons. For example, a fifty-cent coupon towards coffee now counts as a dollar. Two things to remember: the value of the coupon can never exceed the price of the product, so don't squander coupons for which you can't get "change" or credit; if the coupon entitles you to a free product, you will *not* get a duplicate, again because the value of the coupon cannot be more than the product. If your supermarket never has double coupon days, then you should watch for supermarket specials before cashing fifty-cent coupons, unless you really need the items.

Personally, I set a limit of fifty cents and never send for cash refunds below that amount. I don't use this rule for coupons for free merchandise. Spiraling inflation causes money to decrease in value as coupons become worth their weight in gold. Nana had eight brothers and sisters, so her mother had to find nourishing and filling meals that would satisfy her growing brood. She concentrated on economical rice, pasta, and potato combinations, but today even those items are high priced. A coupon for a box of Minute Rice® is worth twice as much as a fifty-cent cash refund. If the value of the coupon at mailing date is under my half-dollar limit, I still request the coupon rebate. Sometimes by the time the mailman delivers ny return or time elapses before I actually redeem it at the store, the coupon has increased substantially in value. Never skip small coupons believing they are insignificant, because they could represent chunky rewards.

People often ask if I can actually do a full week's grocery shopping and leave my pocketbook at home. Definitely, yes! However, I must bring my chubby coupon organizer and try to steer clear of highly taxed items. State sales taxes must always be paid at the store. The only tax rebate I have ever heard about is from your individual income tax return. Refunds themselves are not taxable as income since they represent gifts from the manufacturers. The only tax you pay is sales tax that you would be responsible for if you actually paid cash for the item.

Now you have learned my priceless secret. That's how I purchased $120 worth of groceries for merely $.79. I used free coupons for specific products or grocery items of my choice, such as fresh fruit, vegetables, cheese, and meat. The $.79 covered the sales tax requirements which the state of New Jersey imposes upon toilet paper, paper towels, tissues, and other nonfood items.

By now you realize you must alter your shopping habits to exclude store brands and concentrate on major brand items. Perhaps some day soon, store- and manufacturers will jump on the refunding bandwagon, but right now you will find brands such as these in my shopping cart: Green Giant®, Del Monte®, Libby®, Birds Eye®, Kleenex® and Marcal® paper products, Maxwell House® coffee, Kellogg's® and Post® cereals, Johnson's® and Pampers® disposable diapers, La Choy® and Chun King® Chinese foods,

Pillsbury® and Betty Crocker® cake mixes and frost
ings, Sara Lee® and Pepperidge Farm® frozen des
serts, Cool Whip® nondairy whipped topping, Jell-O
and Royal® desserts, Dr. Pepper®, Pepsi-Cola®, Tab
and 7-Up® soft drinks, Ragu® spaghetti sauce, all Proc
ter and Gamble products, and an occasional bottle of
champagne. That's right, liquor is the most recen
entry in the race for the refunding dollar—a jug of
wine, a loaf of bread, a piece of cheese, and all for the
price of a refund. Is it worth the price of postage? That
is your decision.

Now I'd like to tell you a story about our family
pets. Sandy, the cat, is a true refunder, willing to enjo
new brands of cat food whether they be moist meal,
dry food, or canned combinations of all sorts. Skippy
our Pekinese, refuses to switch brands and will hold ou
for his favorite burger-type dog food. Recently a bran
of cat food offered an interesting refund. If your ca
liked the taste of the food, you could get a refund for tw
free cans by trying only one. However, if your cat hate
the brand, you could receive your total purchase price
plus postage completely refunded. How could any ca
lover refuse to make the test? Well, I had a littl
problem. Before Sandy had a chance to sniff th
contents, our Pekinese gulped down the entire ca
while the confused cat sat in the background. I re
quested the two free cans since Skippy, the unintende
consumer, preferred cat food to his own favorite bran
of dog food. I was fortunate because after cashing m
coupon for two cans, the company had another, simila
promotion with a new box number and new closin
date. This time I separated the Pekinese and the cat s
that Sandy could sample the bill of fare.

Nancy Makarenko

:ippy, who swears off dog food, never gives Sandy, the cat,
chance at the cat food taste test. Does Sandy or doesn't
e??? I don't know.

Don't assume your family won't like fancy vegeta-
es such as pea pods and water chestnuts until you try
em. I never force my family to eat vegetables.
sually, when they see me savor broccoli or asparagus
·ears in butter sauce, they eagerly taste them. They
·n't always like all vegetables as I do, but refunding
fords the opportunity to introduce their taste buds to
·getables that may have remained too expensive for
eryday meals.

Saving money is not the only benefit of refunding.
is emotional therapy that encourages positive think-
g as you overcome the uncertainty of mailing that
·st envelope. Coins continue to roll in, building your
lf-confidence and character as you realize you are
king an active role in helping your family eat better
eals while keeping a strict food budget. Refunding is

both a constructive use of leisure time and a relaxati
guaranteed to lift you from those shopping doldrum
No matter how physically exhausted you become, y
always eagerly participate in the refunding game. I
rest and relaxation to many.

Please play the game by the rules. Don't rip off b
tops in the supermarket. Buy the product and enjoy
then send for your fair share of coupons. Don't abu
the privilege of refunding, which only results in killi
the golden goose. Abide by the rules and overcome t
one-to-a-customer syndrome legally and with inte
rity. Seek additional offers when your labels a
gathering dust. For example, Pillsbury® has so ma
offers available for their ready-to-bake biscuits in
multitude of sizes and variations that my labels
directly from refrigerator to envelope without ev
entering the label file. These are all separate refun
that you are encouraged to participate in absolute
free of charge.

There is another special treat that my fami
enjoys in the evening when we watch television. The
always is a free pizza in the freezer ready to be popp
into the oven, but it's always a different brand. Piz
manufacturers are extremely generous in offeri
money back and free coupons.

The beauty of refunding is that everyone ca
participate, whether you want to toss a quick-and-ea
pizza in the oven or prefer to knead your own dough
my grandmother did. Grandma liked adding her ov
special sauce and chopped mozzarella. (If she packag
it, I'd buy it without a refund.) Today's packaged piz
crusts ready to be rolled are delicious and free for t
asking.

Even persons on special weight reduction, sa

ee, or low-cholesterol diets can refund. Natural foods
agazines, *Prevention*, and other specialized pub-
cations print refund offers. Tasti-Diet, Weight
Vatchers, low-cholesterol salad oils and margarines,
ugar substitutes, salt substitutes, over-the-counter
rugs, cosmetics, and all paper products have refunds.

Refunds are available on practically every product
old. Some offers are available for a limited period of
me, but others have been running for years and are
ill open indefinitely. You may collect a week's grocery
oney per month or even more, depending upon how
ou work at it. Learn which items are refundable, and
clude them on your weekly shopping list. Try to buy
ly refundable items, but when this is impossible, save
labels on speculation for future rebates. Companies
at have offered refund promotions in the past will
fer bigger promotions in the future. When you
ready have the labels in your treasure trove, you
llect immediately.

The latest trend has been for a wider range of
fund possibilities with increased value for each if you
mbine products. For example, the sponsor may list
x items in a mix-or-match promotion. You can try one
more for fifty cents back on each. However, should
u decide to try all six, you will receive a bonus dollar
ck in addition to fifty cents for each product used,
inging your total to four dollars. Sometimes you
erely have to refer to your code number index file and
sh-register-tape folder to come up with one or two
oducts, so you are well on your way to accomplishing
e entire special refund offer. The cost of postage is
inor compared with a four-dollar cash offer. How-
er, don't forget to include it in your record keeping
r an actual accounting of profits reaped.

Remember, don't let the big ones get away! M
brother, Pat, bought Nana a Norelco® coffee maker f
Christmas, which she really loved. She also enjoyed
surprise, after-Christmas gift of a five-dollar reba
check received weeks later. Pat gave Nana two gifts f
the price of one.

Mom decided to reinvest her toy and batter
refunds into additional toys for the grandchildre
"Refunding sure takes the sting out of shopping," s
announced as she arrived at our house, arms full of to
(also promising refunds). I splurge in luxurious, frost
nail enamels and experiment with ice-cream shades
lip gloss and matching eye shadow. The price is rig
Jim doesn't mind shampoo surprises, but I reser
strawberry essence for myself and no-tears shamp
for my son. My sink cabinet is jammed full of
assortment of bathroom cleaners, laundry detergent
fabric softeners, dishwashing lotions, and heavy-du
floor and wall cleaners. Now if only some considera
company would cooperate and offer a robot or maid f
a day. Even refunds have their limit. I guess I could u
cash from refunds to pay for a window-cleaning servic
Jim, are you listening?

March in the right direction to combat inflatio
Gear your weekly menu around refundable item
Patronize companies that offer refunds, and rea
rewards for serving top-quality brands. In refundin
you learn as you earn. Refunding is more than
national pastime, it has become a way of life for the va
network of refunders in the entire nation.

Handicapped persons, those on fixed incomes, an
growing families have written to tell me how refundin
has changed their lives and helped conquer inflatio
Even millionaires like to save money, so refunding h

niversal appeal. The subscribers to *Dollars Daily* are hysicians, pharmacists, accountants, engineers, colge professors, lawyers, teachers, housewives, students, and the unemployed. No matter how high your atus in life or what your current income may be, you ill become angry at one supermarket visit.

Try tinkering with refunding as a lark. You will on stop toying and turn it into a working action plan signed to trim that budget fast. Now my secrets are urs. Start today, and by the way, HAPPY RE-UNDING. Remember, I am always happy to hear om fellow refunders, especially beginners who may ed help getting started. *You can't afford not to fund*, and I am eager to help. If you have any uestions, comments, or problems, just send a SASE ASK THE COUPON QUEEN, P.O. Box 348, akehurst, New Jersey 08733.

Glossary

Refunding Lingo

ardboard Backing: The cardboard behind the pad of refund forms on the store shelves. It usually gives information about how to get the refund without the form. Most of the time they say, "Sorry all forms are gone, but you may still receive your refund by sending the correct qualifiers with your name, address, and ZIP code to the following box number." Or the cardboard backing may indicate an address where you may write for the required refund form. Cardboard backings provide vital information.

sh Deal: Refund form and the correct qualifiers ready to be mailed for a *cash* return.

sh-offs: Coupons usually for seven or ten cents (or more) off a specific product to be redeemed at the store. These may be printed in newspapers, magazines, or flyers, whenever a company makes a promotion.

nts-off Coupons: Cash-offs

ssified: Section of a special-interest refunding periodical, like *Dollars Daily*, reserved for ex-

changing forms or qualifiers. No other ads ar
accepted. These advertisers are not big companie
but are homemakers and career persons involve
in the refunding hobby.

Clearinghouse: Usually the post office box addres
that handles the refund promotion for the sponso
Always mail your refund request to the correct bo
number listed on the refund form itself. This ofte
is a clearinghouse located in El Paso, Texa
Kankakee, Illinois; or St. Paul, Minnesota. Whe
you have a legitimate complaint about nonrecei
of an offer and have kept an accurate record of th
mailing date, register your complaint with th
company (whose address appears on the produ
itself) who will in turn contact the clearinghous
Clearinghouse box numbers usually close after th
expiration date of the offer.

Complete Deal: Refund form and the correct qualifie
ready to be mailed for cash, a free coupon, o
premium gift.

Coupon: A form of scrip that entitles you to a particula
product or item of your choice depending upo
whatever the coupon specifies. For example, th
coupon may declare "one free jar Maxim® coffe
four-ounce size" or another may read "$4.00 off an
grocery purchases."

Dollars Daily: Monthly publication by the Coupo
Queen, listing over 200 new offers available eac
month, with an approximate total of 2,500 offe
annually. Also gives refunding tips, opinion co
umn, classified section, question box, Free For
Club, refunding instructions, and lingo.

Exchange: Trade or swap

Exchanger: Refunding hobbyist offering to trade forms, cash-offs, qualifiers, free or for a small handling fee. A SASE is practically always required.

Expiration Date: Closing date of refund offer. After this date printed on the refund form, your envelope will probably be returned marked "Box Closed." Some offers are printed without an expiration date and may run several years or until supplies are exhausted. Others may say, "Offer expires in 60 days." Usually, these are long-term, dated offers and may be requested for many months or even years.

Form: See Refund Form. In refunding, a money-plus offer, cash-off, or recipe is *not* considered to be a form.

Handling Fee: Small charge requested for the work involved in exchanging forms. Refund forms are never sold. However, since the process of filing, locating, and honoring requests is so time consuming a very small fee may be asked as compensation for labor.

Hang Tag: Refund offer printed on paper collar found around bottle-type products such as beverages, salad dressing, ketchup, fabric softeners, detergents, etc.

Insert Form: Refund form inserted within the product packaging. Look for specially marked packages indicating that a refund form has been included inside the package.

Label: Outer wrapper on canned goods, usually illustrating contents, announcing brand name and item, net weight, ingredients, and other essential information. The term *Label* is loosely used by refunders when referring to any qualifier.

Lingo: Abbreviations and terminology most often utilized by those engaged in the refunding hobby. At first the terms may seem strange, but after awhile they blend into your vocabulary.

LSASE: Large, Self-Addressed, Stamped Envelope. Usually, the white, business-size envelopes will suffice. LSASE does *not* indicate a king-size, brown kraft envelope is required. Save these for mailing bulky qualifiers to sponsors for super refunds.

Magazine Form: Refund form printed in magazines. Magazines catering to any field of interest may produce refund offers. Magazines geared to homemaking, such as *Family Circle*, have a wealth of refund offers printed in each issue.

Mail-in Certificate: Refund form mailed in special promotions. This type of form may be required.

Money-Plus Forms: A form that requires a certain cash outlay plus qualifiers for a premium gift. Beginners often mistake these for refund forms because they are also placed on supermarket shelves alongside refund offers. Most refunders do not participate in money-plus offers, which may or may not be a bargain. Never send money-plus offers in an exchange for refund offers unless you plainly mark them as extras. Money-plus forms are *not* refund offers.

"Must" Form: Certificate required to receive a refund. Sometimes the form states "This required certificate must accompany your refund request." Only time and experience will tell which "must" forms are actually needed and which companies will honor your request even though this statement appears on the form.

NCD: No Closing Date

NED: No Expiration Date

Newspaper Form: Refund form printed in the newspaper, usually in the Wednesday or Thursday editions with supermarket specials of the week or in Sunday supplements.

No Closing Date: Form does not declare an expiration date. Offers without closing dates may run for a very brief period or until the supply of the premium is exhausted. Some are long standing and still open.

No Limit: Order all you want, but mail separately. Not limited to one request per address or household.

Order All You Want: Send your requests for any quantity with appropriate qualifiers, each in one envelope.

POP: A refunding abbreviation used for Proof of Purchase

POP seal: Proof of Purchase seal often found on cookies, cereal, candy, beverages, paper products, and other items. It usually says, "Proof of Purchase seal" or other descriptive words such as "Quality seal."

Proof of Purchase: Whatever the refund offer specifies as evidence that you purchased the product. It may vary from ingredient panel, net weight designation, proof of purchase seal, box top, box bottom, universal product code, certain wording on the package, cash register tape, code number, or entire label. The offer should state exactly what proof of purchase is required. The proof of purchase is also called the qualifier.

Qualifier: Same as proof of purchase

Rebate: Dollars returned by manufacturer after the purchase of items, such as electrical appliances. These can range in value from two or five dollars for a toaster, hair dryer, or blender to several hundred dollars for an automobile, diamond, or cruise ticket.

Refund Form: Slip of paper found in stores, newspapers, magazines, or specially marked packages that advise of an offer from the company to award cash, coupons, or free gifts for certain proofs of purchase, when mailed to the address printed on the form.

Refunding: The process of sending labels, box tops, and other proofs of purchase to the company or clearinghouse for cash returns, gifts, or coupons for free merchandise.

Refusal Notice: A printed form letter received from the company or clearinghouse advising you that they will not send the refund for a special reason. Usually the reason is specified, and you may sometimes correctly resubmit your request to receive the refund. If the offer has expired by the

----

time you receive the refusal notice, the sponsor usually lists a new address and asks that you return the refusal notice with the correct qualifiers when you mail it to the new address. All refunders get an occasional refusal notice because we are all human, and mistakes do happen. Most of the time you will have your labels and refund form returned, so the error has only cost a postage stamp.

Rejection: Refusal notice

Required Forms: When the refund offer is printed in *Dollars Daily* and states "required," it means the actual refund form containing the information stated that the form was required. However, you may sometimes receive the refund without the form even though the original form specified "required." Try sending without the form. Remember, Columbus took a chance.

Round Robins: Several refunders in different areas exchanging with each other by mail. Each robin is unique, according to the rules of the refunders themselves. For example, a robin may contain twenty-five refund offers mailed in sequence to the same traders in the robin. Each refunder may take as many forms out of the envelopes that they can use, replacing the same number with their own extras, always keeping the total of twenty-five. Usually a designated refunder will assume the responsibility of removing soon to expire forms or freshening the entire envelope on occasion so that the round robin will always be new and inviting.

SASE: Self-addressed, stamped envelope. If you are a new refunder, this is the first abbreviation you must learn to use. If the ad in the classified section requires a SASE, please submit one, or you may not receive a response. Exchangers receive such a large volume of responses to their ads that they could not afford to pay all outgoing postage in such quantity. For the person sending the request to trade forms, it is only one envelope and postage stamp. Also be sure you have applied sufficient postage, since postage-due letters may be refused.

Shuffling Fee: Handling Fee. There should be no payment for actual forms or qualifiers. It is illegal.

Sponsor: Manufacturer offering the refund promotion.

Store Form: Refund form found on supermarket shelves, automotive departments, appliance centers, pharmacies, restaurants, cosmetic departments, specialty shops, shoe stores, yarn shops, everywhere you shop.

Universal Product Code: Small square containing a series of lines and the product number, now appearing on all packaging at the supermarket.

UPC: Universal Product Code

Write-up: *Not* a refund form. The actual newspaper or magazine announcement printed *about* the refund offer. It may direct you to mail qualifiers to the company or clearinghouse address or advise about forthcoming store displays featuring the upcoming promotion.

Appendix

Address Abbreviations

The following two-letter abbreviations for states and territories have been approved by the U.S. Postal Service and are often used today on refund offers and in ads placed in the classified section of *Dollars Daily*. Do not try to spell out the entire state's name when an abbreviation is utilized, unless you are certain that you know which state's name is being abbreviated. You can play it safe by copying the exact address, and if a state abbreviation is given, use it. Don't forget to include the ZIP code on both mailing and return addresses.

Alabama	AL	Delaware	DE
Alaska	AK	District of	
Arizona	AZ	Columbia	DC
Arkansas	AR	Florida	FL
American Samoa	AS	Georgia	GA
California	CA	Guam	GU
Canal Zone	CZ	Hawaii	HI
Colorado	CO	Idaho	ID
Connecticut	CT	Illinois	IL

Indiana	IN	North Dakota	ND
Iowa	IA	Ohio	OH
Kansas	KS	Oklahoma	OK
Kentucky	KY	Oregon	OR
Louisiana	LA	Pennsylvania	PA
Maine	ME	Puerto Rico	PR
Maryland	MD	Rhode Island	RI
Massachusetts	MA	South Carolina	SC
Michigan	MI	South Dakota	SD
Minnesota	MN	Tennessee	TN
Mississippi	MS	Trust Territories	TT
Missouri	MO	Texas	TX
Montana	MT	Utah	UT
Nebraska	NE	Vermont	VT
Nevada	NV	Virginia	VA
New Hampshire	NH	Virgin Islands	VI
New Jersey	NJ	Washington	WA
New Mexico	NM	West Virginia	WV
New York	NY	Wisconsin	WI
North Carolina	NC	Wyoming	WY

Trademark List

he following list enumerates the registered trade-
arks and corresponding trademark owners which are
ed in this book.

DOLPH'S is a registered trademark of Adolph's Ltd.

JAX is a registered trademark of Colgate-Palmolive
Company.

LL is a registered trademark of Lever Brothers.

RM & HAMMER is a registered trademark of Arm
& Hammer, a Division of Church and Dwight.

UNT JEMINA is a registered trademark of The
Quaker Oats Company.

UNT MILLIE'S is a registered trademark of Aunt
Millie's Sauces, Inc.

D LO-DOSE is a registered trademark of Becton
Dickenson and Company.

D MICROFINE is a registered trademark of Becton
Dickenson and Company.

D PLASTIPAK is a registered trademark of Becton
Dickenson and Company.

AGGIES is a registered trademark of Colgate-
Palmolive Company.

AND-AIDS is a registered trademark of Johnson &
Johnson.

BETTY CROCKER is a registered trademark of General Mills.

BIRDS EYE is a registered trademark of General Foods Corporation.

BIZ is a registered trademark of Procter & Gamble Company.

BOLD is a registered trademark of Procter & Gamble Company.

BONUS is a registered trademark of Procter & Gamble Company.

BORN BEAUTIFUL is a registered trademark of Clairol, Inc.

BOUNCE is a registered trademark of Procter & Gamble Company.

BOUNTY is a registered trademark of Procter & Gamble Company.

BOUNTY (candy) is a registered trademark of Campbell Soup Company.

BRIGHT & EARLY is a registered trademark of Coca-Cola Company.

BUITONI is a registered trademark of Buitoni Food Corporation.

BUTTERBALL is a registered trademark of Swift's

BUTTER-NUT is a registered trademark of Coca Cola Company.

CAMAY is a registered trademark of Procter & Gamble Company.

CAMPBELL'S is a registered trademark of Campbell Soup Company.

CANADA DRY is a registered trademark of Canada Dry Corporation.

CARLTON is a registered trademark of American Tobacco Company.

ARNATION is a registered trademark of Carnation Company.

ASCADE is a registered trademark of Procter & Gamble Company.

ELENTANO is a registered trademark of Celentano Brothers, Inc.

EPACOL is a registered trademark of Merrell-National Laboratories.

HAP STICK is a registered trademark of Chap Stick Company.

HARMIN is a registered trademark of Procter & Gamble Company.

HEER is a registered trademark of Procter & Gamble Company.

HEX is a registered trademark of Ralston Purina Company.

HIFFON is a registered trademark of Anderson Clayton Foods.

HIPS AHOY! is a registered trademark of Nabisco, Inc.

HUN KING is a registered trademark of RJR Foods, Inc.

LAIRESS is a registered trademark of Clairol, Inc.

OAST is a registered trademark of Procter & Gamble Company.

OLGATE is a registered trademark of Colgate-Palmolive Company.

OMET is a registered trademark of Procter & Gamble Company.

OOL WHIP is a registered trademark of General Foods Corporation.

ORNING WARE is a registered trademark of Corning Glass Works.

COUNTRY TIME is a registered trademark General Foods Corporation.

CRACKER JACK is a registered trademark Cracker Jack, a division of Borden Foods.

CREAMETTE'S is a registered trademark of Th Creamette Company.

CREMORA is a registered trademark of Borde Foods.

CREST is a registered trademark of Procter Gamble Company.

CRICKET LIGHTERS is a registered trademark The Gillette Company.

CRISCO is a registered trademark of Procter Gamble Company.

CRUNCHOLA is a registered trademark of Sunfie Foods.

CUBEX is a registered trademark of Cubex.

CURITY GUARD is a registered trademark Colgate-Palmolive Company.

CYCLE is a registered trademark of General Foo Corporation.

DASH is a registered trademark of Procter & Gamb Company.

DATRIL is a registered trademark of Bristol-Mye Company.

DAYCARE is a registered trademark of Vic Chemical Company. Richardson-Merrell, Inc.

DAZEY DONUT FACTORY is a registered trad mark of Dazey Company.

DECAF is a registered trademark of The Nest Company.

DEL MONTE is a registered trademark of Del Mon Corporation.

DERMASSAGE is a registered trademark of Colgat Palmolive Company.

EVIL DOGS is a registered trademark of Borden
Foods.

IAL is a registered trademark of Armour Dial, Inc.,
a division of Armour & Company.

ET PEPSI is a registered trademark of Pepsi-Cola
Company.

IXIES is a registered trademark of Dixie Paper
Company, Inc.

R. PEPPER is a registered trademark of Dr. Pepper
Company.

OLE is a registered trademark of Castle & Cooke
Foods.

OW BATHROOM CLEANER is a registered trademark of the Dow Chemical Company.

OWGARD is a registered trademark of the Dow
Chemical Company.

OWNY is a registered trademark of Procter &
Gamble Company.

RAKES is a registered trademark of Drake Bakeries
Inc.

REFT is a registered trademark of Procter & Gamble
Company.

ULANY is a registered trademark of Dulany Foods,
Inc., a subsidiary of United Foods Inc.

UNCAN HINES is a registered trademark of
Procter & Gamble Company.

UZ is a registered trademark of Procter & Gamble
Company.

ARTH BORN is a registered trademark of the
Gillette Company.

FERDENT is a registered trademark of Warner-
Lambert Company.

RA is a registered trademark of Procter & Gamble
Company.

EVEREADY is a registered trademark of Unio Carbide Consumer Products.

FLUFFO is a registered trademark of Procter Gamble Company.

FLUORIGARD is a registered trademark of Colgate Palmolive Company.

FOLGER'S is a registered trademark of Procter Gamble Company.

FORMULA 44 is a registered trademark of Vick Health Care Division, Richardson-Merrell, Inc.

FORMULA 44-D is a registered trademark of Vick Health Care Division, Richardson-Merrell, Inc.

FRENCH'S is a registered trademark of R. T. Frenc Company.

FRESHEN-UP is a registered trademark of Warner Lambert Company.

FRISKIES is a registered trademark of Carnatio Company.

FRUIT LOOPS is a registered trademark of Th Kellogg Company.

FUNNY FACE is a registered trademark of Pillsbur Company.

GAIN is a registered trademark of Procter & Gamb Company.

GAINES is a registered trademark of General Foo Corporation.

GAS MISER is a registered trademark of Unio Carbide Corporation.

GLAD is a registered trademark of Union Carbic Corporation.

GLEEM is a registered trademark of Procter Gamble Company.

GOLD MEDAL is a registered trademark of Gener Mills, Inc.

OOD HUMOR is a registered trademark of The Good Humor Corporation.

ORTON'S is a registered trademark of The Gorton Corporation, a subsidiary of General Mills, Inc.

REEN GIANT is a registered trademark of Green Giant Company.

AMILTON BEACH is a registered trademark of Hamilton Beach Company, a division of Scovill Manufacturing.

ANDI-WRAP is a registered trademark of The Dow Chemical Company.

ARVEST AMBER is a registered trademark of Anchor Hocking Corporation.

AWAIIAN PUNCH is a registered trademark of RJR Foods Inc.

EAD AND SHOULDERS is a registered trademark of Procter & Gamble Company.

EFTY is a registered trademark of Mobil Chemical Company.

EINZ is a registered trademark of H.J. Heinz Company.

-C is a registered trademark of Coca-Cola Company.

OLLOWAY HOUSE is a registered trademark of Green Giant Company.

OTEL BAR is a registered trademark of Hotel Bar Foods, Inc.

OWARD JOHNSON is a registered trademark of Howard Johnson's Grocery Products.

UNT'S is a registered trademark of Hunt-Wesson Foods, Inc.

YGRADE is a registered trademark of Hygrade.

ISTAMATIC is a registered trademark of Eastman Kodak Company.

ORY is a registered trademark of Procter & Gamble Company.

JELL-O is a registered trademark of General Foo~
    Corporation.

JERGEN'S is a registered trademark of The Andre~
    Jergens Company, a subsidiary of Americ~
    Brands, Inc.

JETCLEAN is a registered trademark of Mayt~
    Company.

JIF is a registered trademark of Procter & Gaml~
    Company.

JOHN'S is a registered trademark of Anthony J. Piz~
    Food Products Corporation.

JOHNSON & JOHNSON is a registered trademark
    Johnson & Johnson.

JOHNSON'S is a registered trademark of Robert
    Johnston Company, Inc., a subsidiary of Wa~
    Foods Company.

JOY is a registered trademark of Procter & Gaml~
    Company.

KELLOGG'S is a registered trademark of The Kello~
    Company.

KENNER is a registered trademark of Kenn~
    Products, a division of General Mills Fun Gro~
    Inc.

KLEEN KITTY is a registered trademark of Superi~
    Pet Products, Inc.

KLEENEX is a registered trademark of Kimber~
    Clark Corporation.

KOOL SUPER LIGHTS is a registered trademark
    Brown and Williamson Tobacco Company.

KOOL-AID is a registered trademark of Gene~
    Foods Corporation.

KORDITE is a registered trademark of Mo~
    Chemical Company.

KOSCIVSKO is a registered trademark of Pride of t~
    Family Products Company.

KRISPY CRACKERS is a registered trademark of Sunshine Biscuit Company.

LaCHOY is a registered trademark of LaChoy Food Products, a division of Beatrice Foods Company.

LA ROSA is a registered trademark of V. Lakosa & Sons, Inc.

LAND O' LAKES is a registered trademark of Land O'Lakes, Inc.

LAVA is a registered trademark of Procter & Gamble Company.

LAVORIS is a registered trademark of Vick Chemical Company.

LAWRY'S is a registered trademark of Lawry's Foods Inc.

LEE is a registered trademark of Battery Systems, Inc.

LENDER'S is a registered trademark of Lender's Bagel Bakery, Inc.

LIBBY'S is a registered trademark of Libby, McNeill & Libby.

LILT is a registered trademark of Procter & Gamble Company.

LISTERINE is a registered trademark of Warner-Lambert Company.

LISTERMINT is a registered trademark of Warner-Lambert Company.

LOLLI-PUPS is a registered trademark of Hi-Life Packing Company.

LUVS is a registered trademark of Procter & Gamble Company.

LUX is a registered trademark of Lever Brothers Company.

MAN-POWER is a registered trademark of Shulton, Inc.

MARCAL is a registered trademark of Marcal Paper Mills, Inc.

MARIE'S is a registered trademark of Specialty Brands, Inc.

MAXIM is a registered trademark of Maxwell House.

MAXWELL HOUSE is a registered trademark of Maxwell House.

MEOW MIX is a registered trademark of Ralston Purina.

MINOLTA is a registered trademark of Minolta Corporation.

MINUTE MAID is a registered trademark of Coca-Cola Company.

MINUTE RICE is a registered trademark of General Foods Corporation.

MISS CLAIROL is a registered trademark of Clairol, Inc.

MORNINGSTAR FARMS is a registered trademark of Miles Laboratories.

MR. CLEAN is a registered trademark of Procter & Gamble Company.

MR. PEANUT and the MR. PEANUT figure is a registered trademark of Standard Brands Inc.

MRS. T'S is a registered trademark of Ateeco Inc.

NABISCO is a registered trademark of Nabisco, Inc.

NESCAFÉ is a registered trademark of The Nestlé Company, Inc.

NESTEA is a registered trademark of The Nestlé Company, Inc.

NESTLÉ QUIK is a registered trademark of The Nestlé Company, Inc.

NESTLÉ'S is a registered trademark of The Nestlé Company, Inc.

NEW FREEDOM is a registered trademark of Kimberly-Clark Corporation.

NICE 'N EASY is a registered trademark of Clairol, Inc.

NORELCO is a registered trademark of North American Philips Corporation.

NORELCO SMOKEY is a registered trademark of North American Philips Corporation.

NYQUIL is a registered trademark of Vicks Health Care Division, Richardson-Merrell Inc.

OCTAGON is a registered trademark of Colgate-Palmolive Company.

ORACIN is a registered trademark of Vicks Health Care Division, Richardson-Merrell, Inc.

OREO is a registered trademark of Nabisco, Inc.

OSCAR MAYER is a registered trademark of Oscar Mayer & Company.

OXYDOL is a registered trademark of Procter & Gamble Company.

PAMPERS is a registered trademark of Procter & Gamble Company.

PEPPERIDGE FARM is a registered trademark of Pepperidge Farm, Inc., a subsidiary of Campbell Soup Company.

PEPSI-COLA is a registered trademark of Pepsi-Cola Company.

PILLSBURY is a registered trademark of The Pillsbury Company.

PING-PONG is a registered trademark of Parker Brothers.

PLANTERS is a registered trademark of Standard Brands Inc., Confectionery Division.

POST RAISIN BRAN is a registered trademark of General Foods Corporation.

PRELL is a registered trademark of Procter & Gamble Company.

PRESTOBURGER is a registered trademark of National Presto Industries.

PRESTONE is a registered trademark of Union Carbide Corporation.

PRIDE OF THE FARM is a registered trademark of Hunt-Wesson Foods, Inc.

PRIME is a registered trademark of Union Carbide Corporation.

PRINGLES is a registered trademark of Procter & Gamble Company.

PUFFS is a registered trademark of Procter & Gamble Company.

PUMA is a registered trademark of Beconta Inc.

PURINA is a registered trademark of Ralston Purina Company.

Q-TIPS is a registered trademark of Cheseborough-Pond's.

QUAKER is a registered trademark of The Quaker Oats Company.

RAGÚ is a registered trademark of Ragú Foods, Inc.

RAID is a registered trademark of S. C. Johnson & Son, Inc.

RAIN DANCE is a registered trademark of Dupont Company.

RALEIGH LIGHTS is a registered trademark of Brown and Williamson Tobacco Company.

RALLY is a registered trademark of Dupont Company.

RAPID-SHAVE is a registered trademark of Colgate-Palmolive Company.

RATH is a registered trademark of Rath Packing Company.

RAY-O-VAC is a registered trademark of Ray-O-Vac, a division of ESB Inc.

RED L is a registered trademark of Red L Foods Corporation.

REDDI-WHIP is a registered trademark of Reddi-Whip, Inc.

REDPACK is a registered trademark of California Canners and Growers.

RICH'S is a registered trademark of Rich Food Products.

RIVAL is a registered trademark of Rival Manufacturing Company.

ROYAL is a registered trademark of Standard Brands, Inc.

SAFEGUARD is a registered trademark of Procter & Gamble Company.

SALAD CRISPINS is a registered trademark of Swiss Chalet Food Products.

SALVO is a registered trademark of Procter & Gamble Company.

SANKA is a registered trademark of General Foods Corporation.

SARA LEE is a registered trademark of Kitchens of Sara Lee, Inc.

SARAN WRAP is a registered trademark of the Dow Chemical Company.

SCHICK is a registered trademark of Schick Company.

SCOPE is a registered trademark of Procter & Gamble Company.

SCOTT is a registered trademark of Scott Paper Company.

SCRABBLE is a registered trademark of Selchow & Righter Company.

SECRET is a registered trademark of Procter & Gamble Company.

SEVEN SEAS is a registered trademark of Anderson Clayton Foods.

7-UP is a registered trademark of the Seven Up Company.

SHAKE 'N BAKE is a registered trademark of General Foods Corporation.

SIGNAL is a registered trademark of Lever Brothers Company.

SIMONIZ is a registered trademark of Dupont Company.

SKIL is a registered trademark of Skil Corporation.

SKITTLE'S is a registered trademark of Mars, Inc.

SKOTCH is a registered trademark of Hamilton-Skotch Corporation.

SNACK PAK is a registered trademark of Hunt-Wesson Foods Inc.

SPECIAL DINNERS is a registered trademark of Ralston Purina Company.

SPIC AND SPAN is a registered trademark of Procter & Gamble Company.

SPRINKLE SWEET is a registered trademark of Pillsbury Company.

SQUARE MEAL is a registered trademark of Star-Kist Foods, Inc.

SUCCESS is a registered trademark of Riviana Goods, Inc.

SUN LITE is a registered trademark of Sunlite Food Products Company, Inc.

SUNBEAM is a registered trademark of Sunbeam Corporation.

SURE is a registered trademark of Procter & Gamble Company.

TAB is a registered trademark of Coca-Cola Company.

TASTE O'SEA is a registered trademark of O'Donnell-Usen Fisheries Corporation.

TASTI-DIET is a registered trademark of Tillie Lewis Foods, Inc.

TENDER VITTLES is a registered trademark of Ralson Purina Company.

TERI is a registered trademark of Kimberly-Clark Corporation.

THANK YOU BRAND is a registered trademark of Michigan Fruit Canners, Inc.

THRILL is a registered trademark of Procter & Gamble Company.

TIDE is a registered trademark of Procter & Gamble Company.

TOP JOB is a registered trademark of Procter & Gamble Company.

TOYOTA is a registered trademark of Toyota Motor Sales, USA, Inc.

TUFF STUFF is a registered trademark of Union Carbide Corporation.

ULTRA BRITE is a registered trademark of Colgate-Palmolive Company.

UNDERWOOD is a registered trademark of William Underwood Company.

VA-TRO-NOL is a registered trademark of Vicks Health Care Division, Richardson-Merrell, Inc.

VANISH is a registered trademark of The Drackett Company.

VAPOSTEAM is a registered trademark of Vicks Health Care Division, Richardson-Merrell, Inc.

VEG-ALL is a registered trademark of The Larsen Company.

VERA is a registered trademark of Crown Zellerbach Corporation.

VICKS is a registered trademark of Vicks Health Care Division, Richardson-Merrell, Inc.

VICKS MEDI-TRATING is a registered trademark of of Vicks Health Care Division, Richardson-Merrell, Inc.

VICKS VAPORUB is a registered trademark of Vicks Health Care Division, Richardson-Merrell, Inc.

VICTORS is a registered trademark of Vicks Health Care Division, Richardson-Merrell, Inc.

WALDORF is a registered trademark of Scott Paper Company.

WEIGHT WATCHERS is a registered trademark of Weight Watchers International Inc.

WELCH'S is a registered trademark of Welch Foods, Inc.

WHITE CLOUD is a registered trademark of Procter & Gamble Company.

WINNER is a registered trademark of Kodak Company.

WONDRA is a registered trademark of Procter & Gamble Company.

WYLER'S is a registered trademark of Wyler Foods/ Borden Inc.

YODELS is a registered trademark of Borden Foods.

ZEST is a registered trademark of Procter & Gamble Company.

ZIPLOC is a registered trademark of the Dow Chemical Company.